Soups

Recipes to make your own gifts

Use these recipes to delight your friends and family. Each recipe includes gift tags for your convenience — just cut them out and personalize!

To decorate jars, cut fabric in 9" diameter circles. Screw down the jar ring to hold fabric in place or hold fabric with a ribbon, raffia, twine, yarn, lace, or string (first secure the fabric with a rubber band before tying). Punch a hole into the corner of the tag and use the ribbon, raffia, twine, yarn, lace, or string to attach the tag to the jar.

These gifts should keep for up to six months.

Made in China

Second Edition

Distributed By:

507 Industrial Street
Waverly, IA 50677

ISBN 1-56383-124-4
Item #3004

Rainbow Bean Soup Mix

3/4 C. dried red beans
3/4 C. Great Northern beans
3/4 C. split peas
3/4 C. lentils, preferably
   red or yellow
3/4 C. black beans

Seasoning Packet:

2 T. dried minced onion
2 T. beef bouillon granules
2 T. dried parsley flakes
2 tsp. dried basil
2 tsp. powdered lemonade
   mix with sugar
1 1/2 tsp. chili powder
1 tsp. pepper
1 tsp. dried oregano

Layer the beans in the order given into a wide-mouth 1-quart canning jar. Mix and place the seasonings in a small plastic bag. Place the packet on top of the beans.

Attach a gift tag with the cooking directions.

Rainbow Bean Soup

1 jar Rainbow Bean Soup Mix
1 (28 ounce) can crushed
tomatoes

Remove seasoning packet from Rainbow Bean Soup Mix and set aside. Rinse beans and place in microwave safe dish. Cover with water, 1 to 2 inches over top of beans. Cover dish loosely with plastic wrap and microwave on high for 15 minutes, rotating after 7 minutes. Drain and rinse beans very well. Place beans in a large soup pot. Add 8 cups water, cover and bring to a boil. Lower heat, cover and simmer 1 hour or until beans are tender. Stir occasionally. Add tomatoes and seasoning packet and simmer for another 1/2 hour.

Rainbow Bean Soup

1 jar Rainbow Bean Soup Mix   1 (28 ounce) can crushed
tomatoes

Remove seasoning packet from Rainbow Bean Soup Mix and set aside. Rinse beans and place in microwave safe dish. Cover with water, 1 to 2 inches over top of beans. Cover dish loosely with plastic wrap and microwave on high for 15 minutes, rotating after 7 minutes. Drain and rinse beans very well. Place beans in a large soup pot. Add 8 cups water, cover and bring to a boil. Lower heat, cover and simmer 1 hour or until beans are tender. Stir occasionally. Add tomatoes and seasoning packet and simmer for another 1/2 hour.

Rainbow Bean Soup

1 jar Rainbow Bean Soup Mix   1 (28 ounce) can crushed
tomatoes

Remove seasoning packet from Rainbow Bean Soup Mix and set aside. Rinse beans and place in microwave safe dish. Cover with water, 1 to 2 inches over top of beans. Cover dish loosely with plastic wrap and microwave on high for 15 minutes, rotating after 7 minutes. Drain and rinse beans very well. Place beans in a large soup pot. Add 8 cups water, cover and bring to a boil. Lower heat, cover and simmer 1 hour or until beans are tender. Stir occasionally. Add tomatoes and seasoning packet and simmer for another 1/2 hour.

Rainbow Bean Soup

1 jar Rainbow Bean Soup Mix   1 (28 ounce) can crushed
tomatoes

Remove seasoning packet from Rainbow Bean Soup Mix and set aside. Rinse beans and place in microwave safe dish. Cover with water, 1 to 2 inches over top of beans. Cover dish loosely with plastic wrap and microwave on high for 15 minutes, rotating after 7 minutes. Drain and rinse beans very well. Place beans in a large soup pot. Add 8 cups water, cover and bring to a boil. Lower heat, cover and simmer 1 hour or until beans are tender. Stir occasionally. Add tomatoes and seasoning packet and simmer for another 1/2 hour.

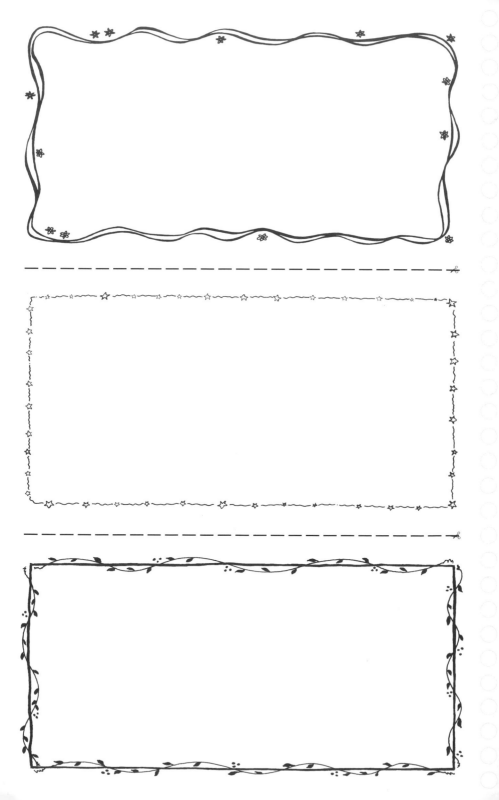

Rainbow Bean Soup

1 jar Rainbow Bean Soup Mix   1 (28 ounce) can crushed
                                              tomatoes

    Remove seasoning packet from Rainbow Bean Soup Mix and set aside. Rinse beans and place in microwave safe dish. Cover with water, 1 to 2 inches over top of beans. Cover dish loosely with plastic wrap and microwave on high for 15 minutes, rotating after 7 minutes. Drain and rinse beans very well. Place beans in a large soup pot. Add 8 cups water, cover and bring to a boil. Lower heat, cover and simmer 1 hour or until beans are tender. Stir occasionally. Add tomatoes and seasoning packet and simmer for another 1/2 hour.

Rainbow Bean Soup

1 jar Rainbow Bean Soup Mix   1 (28 ounce) can crushed
                                              tomatoes

    Remove seasoning packet from Rainbow Bean Soup Mix and set aside. Rinse beans and place in microwave safe dish. Cover with water, 1 to 2 inches over top of beans. Cover dish loosely with plastic wrap and microwave on high for 15 minutes, rotating after 7 minutes. Drain and rinse beans very well. Place beans in a large soup pot. Add 8 cups water, cover and bring to a boil. Lower heat, cover and simmer 1 hour or until beans are tender. Stir occasionally. Add tomatoes and seasoning packet and simmer for another 1/2 hour.

Rainbow Bean Soup

1 jar Rainbow Bean Soup Mix   1 (28 ounce) can crushed
                                              tomatoes

    Remove seasoning packet from Rainbow Bean Soup Mix and set aside. Rinse beans and place in microwave safe dish. Cover with water, 1 to 2 inches over top of beans. Cover dish loosely with plastic wrap and microwave on high for 15 minutes, rotating after 7 minutes. Drain and rinse beans very well. Place beans in a large soup pot. Add 8 cups water, cover and bring to a boil. Lower heat, cover and simmer 1 hour or until beans are tender. Stir occasionally. Add tomatoes and seasoning packet and simmer for another 1/2 hour.

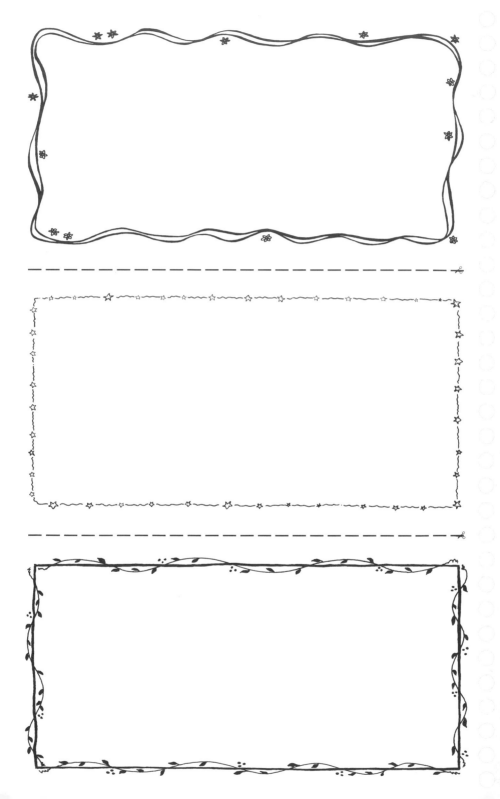

Chicken Noodle Soup Mix

2 T. dried minced onion
2 T. chicken bouillon granules
2 tsp. celery flakes
1 tsp. pepper
4 C. wide egg noodles

Layer the ingredients in the order given into a wide-mouth 1-quart canning jar. Pack each layer in place before adding the next ingredient.

Attach a gift tag with the cooking directions.

Chicken Noodle Soup

1 jar Chicken Noodle Soup Mix
2 (5 ounce) cans chicken

Bring 10 cups of water to a boil in a large soup pot. Add the Chicken Noodle Soup Mix. Add chicken, breaking it up well with a fork. Bring to a boil, lower heat and simmer uncovered for 12 to 15 minutes or until noodles are tender.

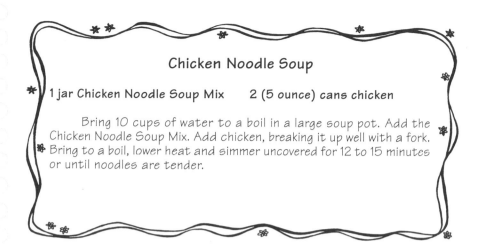

Chicken Noodle Soup

1 jar Chicken Noodle Soup Mix   2 (5 ounce) cans chicken

Bring 10 cups of water to a boil in a large soup pot. Add the Chicken Noodle Soup Mix. Add chicken, breaking it up well with a fork. Bring to a boil, lower heat and simmer uncovered for 12 to 15 minutes or until noodles are tender.

Chicken Noodle Soup

1 jar Chicken Noodle Soup Mix   2 (5 ounce) cans chicken

Bring 10 cups of water to a boil in a large soup pot. Add the Chicken Noodle Soup Mix. Add chicken, breaking it up well with a fork. Bring to a boil, lower heat and simmer uncovered for 12 to 15 minutes or until noodles are tender.

Chicken Noodle Soup

1 jar Chicken Noodle Soup Mix   2 (5 ounce) cans chicken

Bring 10 cups of water to a boil in a large soup pot. Add the Chicken Noodle Soup Mix. Add chicken, breaking it up well with a fork. Bring to a boil, lower heat and simmer uncovered for 12 to 15 minutes or until noodles are tender.

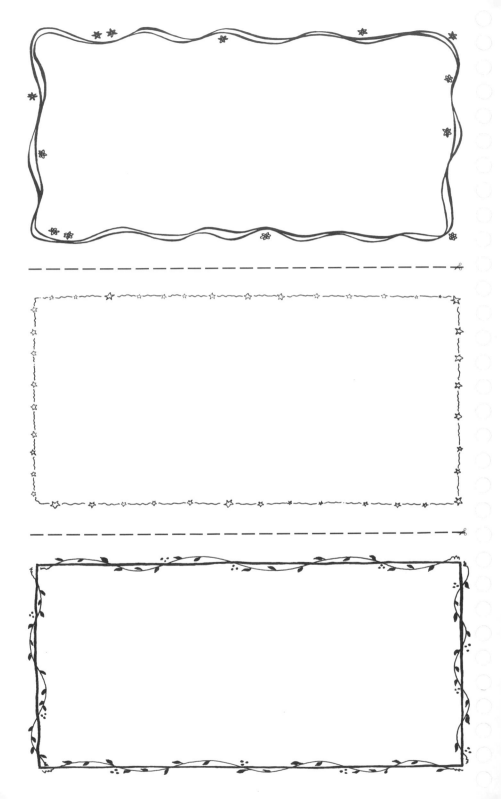

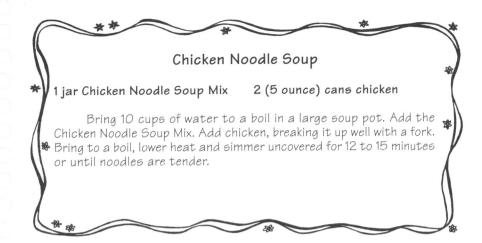

Chicken Noodle Soup

1 jar Chicken Noodle Soup Mix   2 (5 ounce) cans chicken

Bring 10 cups of water to a boil in a large soup pot. Add the Chicken Noodle Soup Mix. Add chicken, breaking it up well with a fork. Bring to a boil, lower heat and simmer uncovered for 12 to 15 minutes or until noodles are tender.

Chicken Noodle Soup

1 jar Chicken Noodle Soup Mix   2 (5 ounce) cans chicken

Bring 10 cups of water to a boil in a large soup pot. Add the Chicken Noodle Soup Mix. Add chicken, breaking it up well with a fork. Bring to a boil, lower heat and simmer uncovered for 12 to 15 minutes or until noodles are tender.

Chicken Noodle Soup

1 jar Chicken Noodle Soup Mix   2 (5 ounce) cans chicken

Bring 10 cups of water to a boil in a large soup pot. Add the Chicken Noodle Soup Mix. Add chicken, breaking it up well with a fork. Bring to a boil, lower heat and simmer uncovered for 12 to 15 minutes or until noodles are tender.

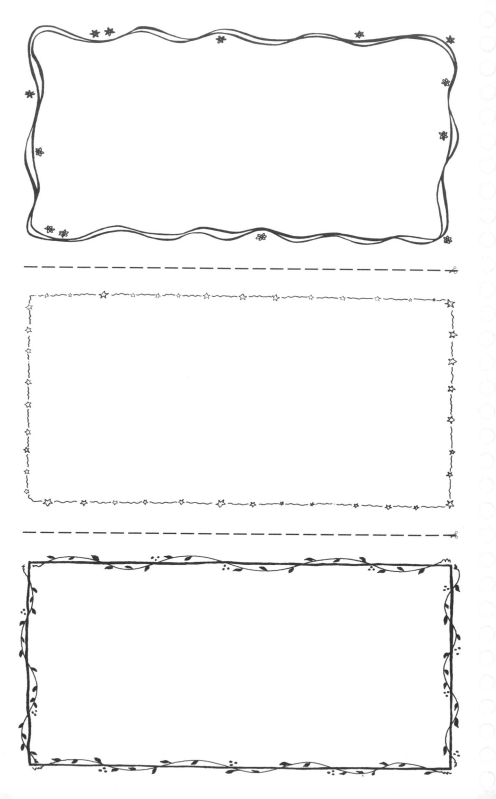

White Bean Chowder Mix

1 2/3 C. dried Great Northern
beans
1 2/3 C. Hungry Jack® instant
potato flakes in a thin
zipper bag

Seasoning Packet:
1/3 C. imitation bacon bits
1/3 C. dried minced onion
2 T. chicken bouillon granules
1 tsp. pepper
1 tsp. sage
1/2 tsp. celery flakes

Layer the ingredients in the order given into a wide-mouth 1-quart canning jar. Mix and place the seasonings in a small plastic bag. Place the packet on top of the bag of potato flakes.

Attach a gift tag with the cooking directions.

White Bean Chowder

1 jar White Bean Chowder Mix
1 (14 ounce) can diced or
crushed tomatoes

Remove seasoning packet and potato flakes bag from White Bean Chowder Mix and set aside. Rinse beans and place in microwave safe dish. Cover with water, 1 to 2 inches over top of beans. Cover dish loosely with plastic wrap and microwave on high for 15 minutes, rotating after 7 minutes. Drain and rinse beans very well. Place beans in a large soup pot. Add 8 cups water, tomatoes and seasoning packet. Cover, bring to a boil. Lower heat, cover and simmer 1 3/4 hours or until beans are tender. Stir in potato flakes.

White Bean Chowder

1 jar White Bean Chowder Mix   1 (14 ounce) can diced or
                                  crushed tomatoes

Remove seasoning packet and potato flakes bag from White Bean Chowder Mix and set aside. Rinse beans and place in microwave safe dish. Cover with water, 1 to 2 inches over top of beans. Cover dish loosely with plastic wrap and microwave on high for 15 minutes, rotating after 7 minutes. Drain and rinse beans very well. Place beans in a large soup pot. Add 8 cups water, tomatoes and seasoning packet. Cover, bring to a boil. Lower heat, cover and simmer 1 3/4 hours or until beans are tender. Stir in potato flakes.

White Bean Chowder

1 jar White Bean Chowder Mix   1 (14 ounce) can diced or
                                  crushed tomatoes

Remove seasoning packet and potato flakes bag from White Bean Chowder Mix and set aside. Rinse beans and place in microwave safe dish. Cover with water, 1 to 2 inches over top of beans. Cover dish loosely with plastic wrap and microwave on high for 15 minutes, rotating after 7 minutes. Drain and rinse beans very well. Place beans in a large soup pot. Add 8 cups water, tomatoes and seasoning packet. Cover, bring to a boil. Lower heat, cover and simmer 1 3/4 hours or until beans are tender. Stir in potato flakes.

White Bean Chowder

1 jar White Bean Chowder Mix   1 (14 ounce) can diced or
                                  crushed tomatoes

Remove seasoning packet and potato flakes bag from White Bean Chowder Mix and set aside. Rinse beans and place in microwave safe dish. Cover with water, 1 to 2 inches over top of beans. Cover dish loosely with plastic wrap and microwave on high for 15 minutes, rotating after 7 minutes. Drain and rinse beans very well. Place beans in a large soup pot. Add 8 cups water, tomatoes and seasoning packet. Cover, bring to a boil. Lower heat, cover and simmer 1 3/4 hours or until beans are tender. Stir in potato flakes.

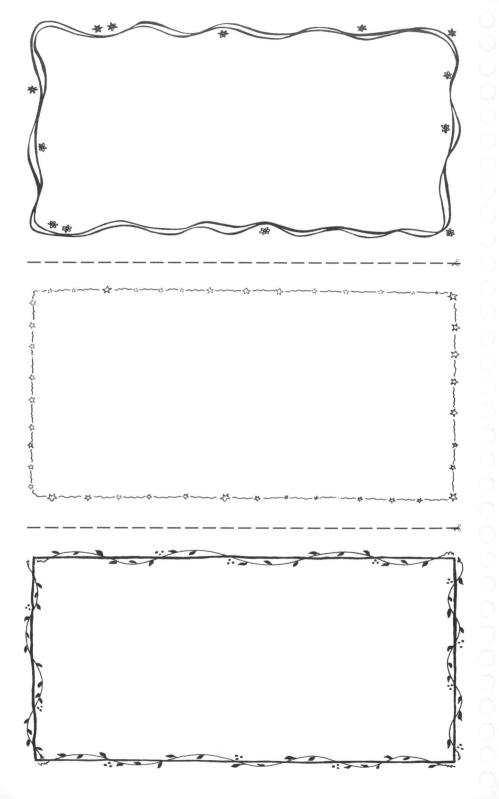

White Bean Chowder

1 jar White Bean Chowder Mix 1 (14 ounce) can diced or
                  crushed tomatoes

  Remove seasoning packet and potato flakes bag from White Bean Chowder Mix and set aside. Rinse beans and place in microwave safe dish. Cover with water, 1 to 2 inches over top of beans. Cover dish loosely with plastic wrap and microwave on high for 15 minutes, rotating after 7 minutes. Drain and rinse beans very well. Place beans in a large soup pot. Add 8 cups water, tomatoes and seasoning packet. Cover, bring to a boil. Lower heat, cover and simmer 1 3/4 hours or until beans are tender. Stir in potato flakes.

White Bean Chowder

1 jar White Bean Chowder Mix 1 (14 ounce) can diced or
                  crushed tomatoes

  Remove seasoning packet and potato flakes bag from White Bean Chowder Mix and set aside. Rinse beans and place in microwave safe dish. Cover with water, 1 to 2 inches over top of beans. Cover dish loosely with plastic wrap and microwave on high for 15 minutes, rotating after 7 minutes. Drain and rinse beans very well. Place beans in a large soup pot. Add 8 cups water, tomatoes and seasoning packet. Cover, bring to a boil. Lower heat, cover and simmer 1 3/4 hours or until beans are tender. Stir in potato flakes.

White Bean Chowder

1 jar White Bean Chowder Mix 1 (14 ounce) can diced or
                  crushed tomatoes

  Remove seasoning packet and potato flakes bag from White Bean Chowder Mix and set aside. Rinse beans and place in microwave safe dish. Cover with water, 1 to 2 inches over top of beans. Cover dish loosely with plastic wrap and microwave on high for 15 minutes, rotating after 7 minutes. Drain and rinse beans very well. Place beans in a large soup pot. Add 8 cups water, tomatoes and seasoning packet. Cover, bring to a boil. Lower heat, cover and simmer 1 3/4 hours or until beans are tender. Stir in potato flakes.

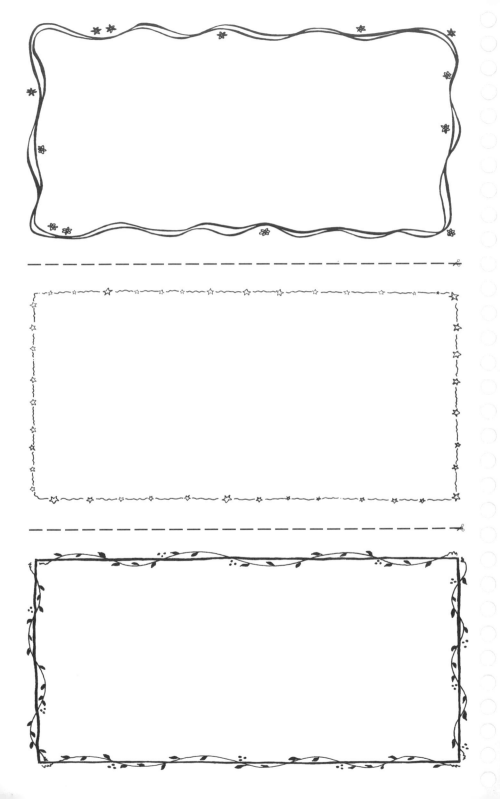

Turkey Noodle Soup Mix

3 T. chicken bouillon granules
1 tsp. pepper
1/2 tsp. dried whole thyme
1/4 tsp. celery seeds
1/4 tsp. garlic powder
1 or 2 bay leaves
4 C. tri-colored spiral pasta

Layer the ingredients in the order given into a wide-mouth 1-quart canning jar. Set the bay leaf against the side of the jar before filling with noodles.

Attach a gift tag with the cooking directions.

A half-yard of fabric should make eight wide-mouth jar covers.

Turkey Noodle Soup

1 jar Turkey Noodle Soup Mix
2 carrots, diced
2 stalks celery, diced
1/4 C. minced onion
3 C. cooked, diced turkey

Place the Turkey Noodle Soup Mix in a large soup pot. Add 12 cups of water. Add the carrots, celery and onion and bring to a boil. Cover, lower heat and simmer for 15 minutes. Discard the bay leaf. Stir in the turkey and simmer an additional 5 minutes.

Turkey Noodle Soup

1 jar Turkey Noodle Soup Mix
2 carrots, diced
2 stalks celery, diced

1/4 C. minced onion
3 C. cooked, diced turkey

Place the Turkey Noodle Soup Mix in a large soup pot. Add 12 cups of water. Add the carrots, celery and onion and bring to a boil. Cover, lower heat and simmer for 15 minutes. Discard the bay leaf. Stir in the turkey and simmer an additional 5 minutes.

Turkey Noodle Soup

1 jar Turkey Noodle Soup Mix
2 carrots, diced
2 stalks celery, diced

1/4 C. minced onion
3 C. cooked, diced turkey

Place the Turkey Noodle Soup Mix in a large soup pot. Add 12 cups of water. Add the carrots, celery and onion and bring to a boil. Cover, lower heat and simmer for 15 minutes. Discard the bay leaf. Stir in the turkey and simmer an additional 5 minutes.

Turkey Noodle Soup

1 jar Turkey Noodle Soup Mix
2 carrots, diced
2 stalks celery, diced

1/4 C. minced onion
3 C. cooked, diced turkey

Place the Turkey Noodle Soup Mix in a large soup pot. Add 12 cups of water. Add the carrots, celery and onion and bring to a boil. Cover, lower heat and simmer for 15 minutes. Discard the bay leaf. Stir in the turkey and simmer an additional 5 minutes.

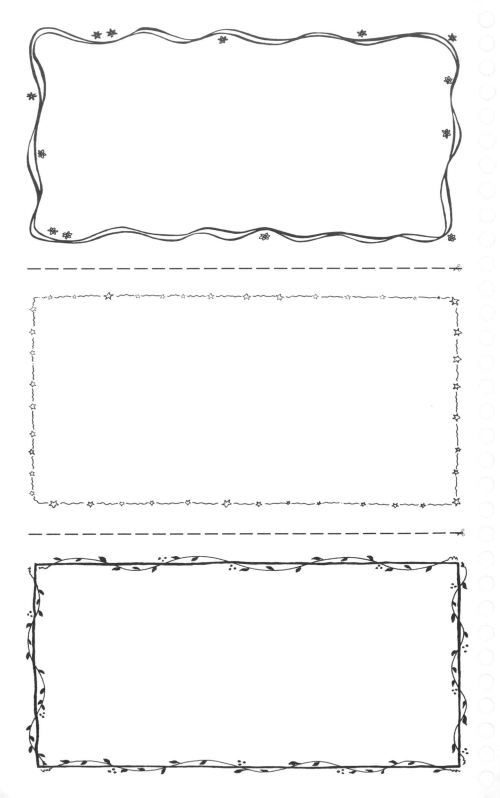

Turkey Noodle Soup

1 jar Turkey Noodle Soup Mix   1/4 C. minced onion
2 carrots, diced   3 C. cooked, diced turkey
2 stalks celery, diced

Place the Turkey Noodle Soup Mix in a large soup pot. Add 12 cups of water. Add the carrots, celery and onion and bring to a boil. Cover, lower heat and simmer for 15 minutes. Discard the bay leaf. Stir in the turkey and simmer an additional 5 minutes.

Turkey Noodle Soup

1 jar Turkey Noodle Soup Mix   1/4 C. minced onion
2 carrots, diced   3 C. cooked, diced turkey
2 stalks celery, diced

Place the Turkey Noodle Soup Mix in a large soup pot. Add 12 cups of water. Add the carrots, celery and onion and bring to a boil. Cover, lower heat and simmer for 15 minutes. Discard the bay leaf. Stir in the turkey and simmer an additional 5 minutes.

Turkey Noodle Soup

1 jar Turkey Noodle Soup Mix   1/4 C. minced onion
2 carrots, diced   3 C. cooked, diced turkey
2 stalks celery, diced

Place the Turkey Noodle Soup Mix in a large soup pot. Add 12 cups of water. Add the carrots, celery and onion and bring to a boil. Cover, lower heat and simmer for 15 minutes. Discard the bay leaf. Stir in the turkey and simmer an additional 5 minutes.

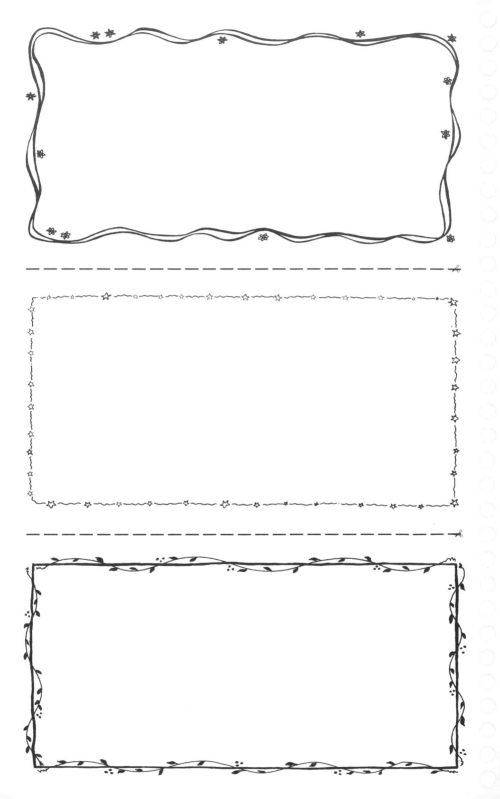

Black-Eyed Pea Soup Mix

3 C. dried black-eyed peas

Seasoning Packet:

1/2 C. dried minced onion
6 T. chicken bouillon granules
2 T. dried parsley flakes
1 T. sugar
2 tsp. dried minced garlic
1 tsp. chili powder
1 tsp. onion powder
1/2 tsp. pepper
1/2 tsp. garlic powder

Place 2 cups of the peas into a wide-mouth 1-quart canning jar. Mix and place the seasonings in a small plastic bag. Place the packet on top of peas. Add the rest of the peas.

Attach a gift tag with the cooking directions.

Black-Eyed Pea Soup

1 jar Black-Eyed Pea Soup Mix
2 (14 ounce) cans diced or
   crushed tomatoes

Remove seasoning packet from Black-Eyed Pea Soup Mix and set aside. Rinse peas and place in microwave safe dish. Cover with water, 1 to 2 inches over top of peas. Cover dish loosely with plastic wrap and microwave on high for 15 minutes, rotating after 7 minutes. Drain and rinse peas very well. Place peas in a large soup pot. Add 10 cups water, tomatoes and seasoning packet. Cover, bring to a boil. Lower heat, cover and simmer 1 1/2 hours or until peas are tender. Stir occasionally.

Black-Eyed Pea Soup

1 jar Black-Eyed Pea Soup Mix   2 (14 ounce) cans diced or
                                                  crushed tomatoes

Remove seasoning packet from Black-Eyed Pea Soup Mix and set aside. Rinse peas and place in microwave safe dish. Cover with water, 1 to 2 inches over top of peas. Cover dish loosely with plastic wrap and microwave on high for 15 minutes, rotating after 7 minutes. Drain and rinse peas very well. Place peas in a large soup pot. Add 10 cups water, tomatoes and seasoning packet. Cover, bring to a boil. Lower heat, cover and simmer 1 1/2 hours or until peas are tender. Stir occasionally.

Black-Eyed Pea Soup

1 jar Black-Eyed Pea Soup Mix   2 (14 ounce) cans diced or
                                                  crushed tomatoes

Remove seasoning packet from Black-Eyed Pea Soup Mix and set aside. Rinse peas and place in microwave safe dish. Cover with water, 1 to 2 inches over top of peas. Cover dish loosely with plastic wrap and microwave on high for 15 minutes, rotating after 7 minutes. Drain and rinse peas very well. Place peas in a large soup pot. Add 10 cups water, tomatoes and seasoning packet. Cover, bring to a boil. Lower heat, cover and simmer 1 1/2 hours or until peas are tender. Stir occasionally.

Black-Eyed Pea Soup

1 jar Black-Eyed Pea Soup Mix   2 (14 ounce) cans diced or
                                                  crushed tomatoes

Remove seasoning packet from Black-Eyed Pea Soup Mix and set aside. Rinse peas and place in microwave safe dish. Cover with water, 1 to 2 inches over top of peas. Cover dish loosely with plastic wrap and microwave on high for 15 minutes, rotating after 7 minutes. Drain and rinse peas very well. Place peas in a large soup pot. Add 10 cups water, tomatoes and seasoning packet. Cover, bring to a boil. Lower heat, cover and simmer 1 1/2 hours or until peas are tender. Stir occasionally.

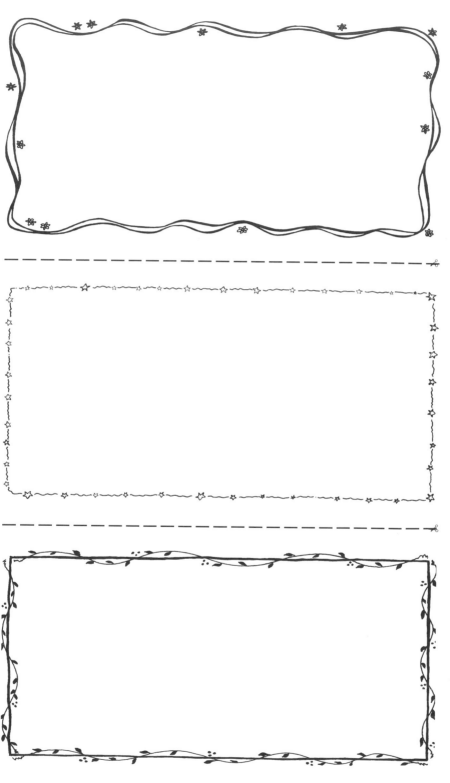

Black-Eyed Pea Soup

1 jar Black-Eyed Pea Soup Mix   2 (14 ounce) cans diced or
                                    crushed tomatoes

Remove seasoning packet from Black-Eyed Pea Soup Mix and set aside. Rinse peas and place in microwave safe dish. Cover with water, 1 to 2 inches over top of peas. Cover dish loosely with plastic wrap and microwave on high for 15 minutes, rotating after 7 minutes. Drain and rinse peas very well. Place peas in a large soup pot. Add 10 cups water, tomatoes and seasoning packet. Cover, bring to a boil. Lower heat, cover and simmer 1 1/2 hours or until peas are tender. Stir occasionally.

Black-Eyed Pea Soup

1 jar Black-Eyed Pea Soup Mix   2 (14 ounce) cans diced or
                                    crushed tomatoes

Remove seasoning packet from Black-Eyed Pea Soup Mix and set aside. Rinse peas and place in microwave safe dish. Cover with water, 1 to 2 inches over top of peas. Cover dish loosely with plastic wrap and microwave on high for 15 minutes, rotating after 7 minutes. Drain and rinse peas very well. Place peas in a large soup pot. Add 10 cups water, tomatoes and seasoning packet. Cover, bring to a boil. Lower heat, cover and simmer 1 1/2 hours or until peas are tender. Stir occasionally.

Black-Eyed Pea Soup

1 jar Black-Eyed Pea Soup Mix   2 (14 ounce) cans diced or
                                    crushed tomatoes

Remove seasoning packet from Black-Eyed Pea Soup Mix and set aside. Rinse peas and place in microwave safe dish. Cover with water, 1 to 2 inches over top of peas. Cover dish loosely with plastic wrap and microwave on high for 15 minutes, rotating after 7 minutes. Drain and rinse peas very well. Place peas in a large soup pot. Add 10 cups water, tomatoes and seasoning packet. Cover, bring to a boil. Lower heat, cover and simmer 1 1/2 hours or until peas are tender. Stir occasionally.

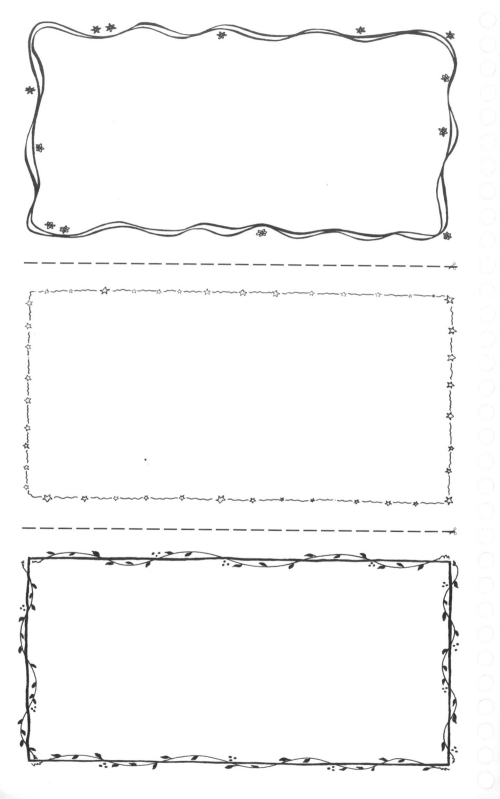

Love Soup Mix

1/3 C. beef bouillon granules
1/4 C. dried minced onion
1/2 C. dried split peas
1/2 C. macaroni
1/4 C. barley
1/2 C. lentils
1/3 C. long-grain white rice
1 C. tri-colored spiral pasta

Layer the ingredients in the order given into a wide-mouth 1-quart canning jar. Pack each layer in place before adding the next ingredient.

Attach a gift tag with the cooking directions.

Love Soup

1 jar Love Soup Mix
1 pound ground beef, browned
and drained

Remove the tri-colored pasta from the Love Soup Mix and set aside. Place the balance of the mix in a large soup pot. Add 12 cups of water. Bring to a boil. Lower heat and simmer for 45 minutes. Add tri-colored pasta, ground beef and simmer 15 minutes more.

Love Soup

1 jar Love Soup Mix

1 pound ground beef, browned and drained

Remove the tri-colored pasta from the Love Soup Mix and set aside. Place the balance of the mix in a large soup pot. Add 12 cups of water. Bring to a boil. Lower heat and simmer for 45 minutes. Add tri-colored pasta, ground beef and simmer 15 minutes more.

Love Soup

1 jar Love Soup Mix

1 pound ground beef, browned and drained

Remove the tri-colored pasta from the Love Soup Mix and set aside. Place the balance of the mix in a large soup pot. Add 12 cups of water. Bring to a boil. Lower heat and simmer for 45 minutes. Add tri-colored pasta, ground beef and simmer 15 minutes more.

Love Soup

1 jar Love Soup Mix

1 pound ground beef, browned and drained

Remove the tri-colored pasta from the Love Soup Mix and set aside. Place the balance of the mix in a large soup pot. Add 12 cups of water. Bring to a boil. Lower heat and simmer for 45 minutes. Add tri-colored pasta, ground beef and simmer 15 minutes more.

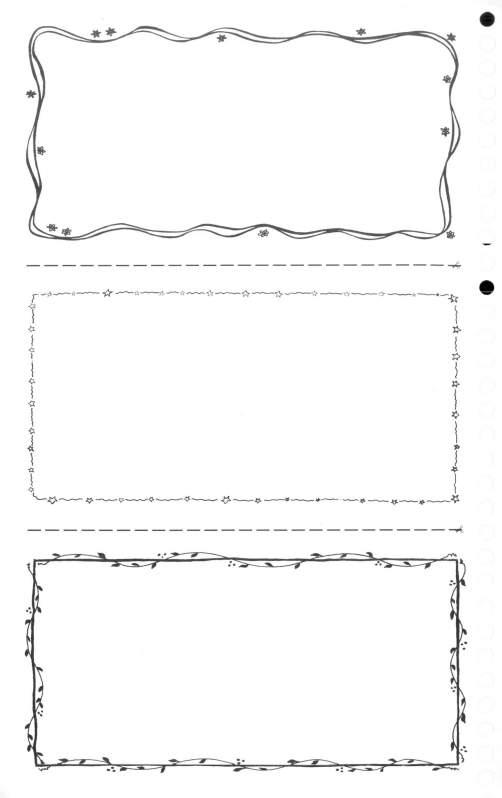

Wild Rice and Barley Soup Mix

1 C. barley
2/3 C. imitation bacon bits
2 T. brown sugar
2 tsp. dried basil
2 tsp. dried oregano
1 tsp. pepper
1 tsp. garlic powder
1 tsp. celery flakes
1/2 C. beef bouillon granules
1 C. wild rice
1 C. dried minced onion

Layer the ingredients in the order given into a wide-mouth 1-quart canning jar. Pack each layer in place before adding the next ingredient.

Attach a gift tag with the cooking directions.

Wild Rice and Barley Soup

1 jar Wild Rice and Barley
    Soup Mix
2 cans sliced mushrooms,
    optional

Place the Wild Rice and Barley Soup Mix in a large soup pot. Add 14 cups of water. Bring to a boil. Add mushrooms if desired. Cover, lower heat and simmer for 1 hour.

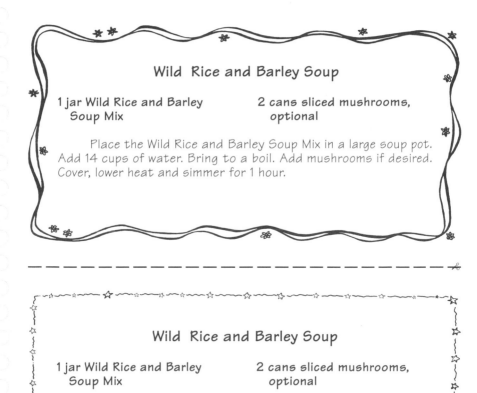

Wild Rice and Barley Soup

1 jar Wild Rice and Barley
  Soup Mix

2 cans sliced mushrooms,
  optional

    Place the Wild Rice and Barley Soup Mix in a large soup pot. Add 14 cups of water. Bring to a boil. Add mushrooms if desired. Cover, lower heat and simmer for 1 hour.

Wild Rice and Barley Soup

1 jar Wild Rice and Barley
  Soup Mix

2 cans sliced mushrooms,
  optional

    Place the Wild Rice and Barley Soup Mix in a large soup pot. Add 14 cups of water. Bring to a boil. Add mushrooms if desired. Cover, lower heat and simmer for 1 hour.

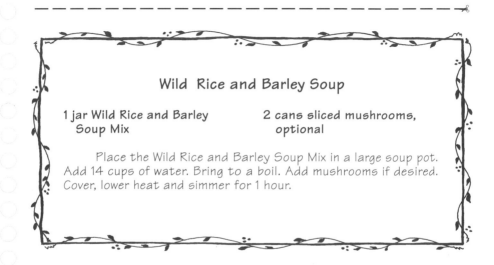

Wild Rice and Barley Soup

1 jar Wild Rice and Barley
  Soup Mix

2 cans sliced mushrooms,
  optional

    Place the Wild Rice and Barley Soup Mix in a large soup pot. Add 14 cups of water. Bring to a boil. Add mushrooms if desired. Cover, lower heat and simmer for 1 hour.

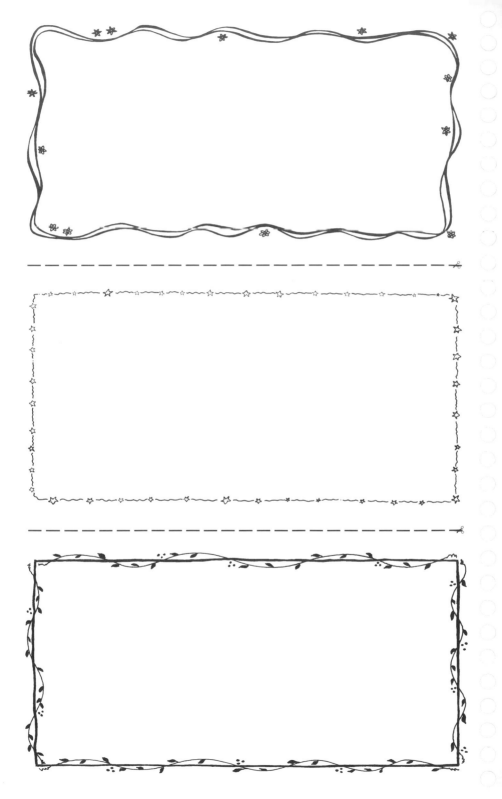

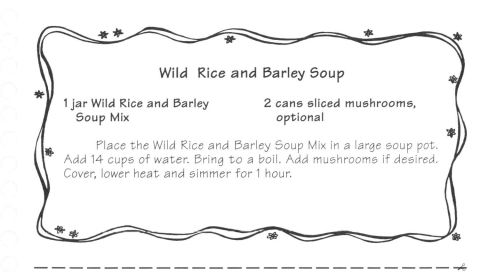

Wild Rice and Barley Soup

1 jar Wild Rice and Barley
Soup Mix

2 cans sliced mushrooms,
optional

Place the Wild Rice and Barley Soup Mix in a large soup pot. Add 14 cups of water. Bring to a boil. Add mushrooms if desired. Cover, lower heat and simmer for 1 hour.

Wild Rice and Barley Soup

1 jar Wild Rice and Barley
Soup Mix

2 cans sliced mushrooms,
optional

Place the Wild Rice and Barley Soup Mix in a large soup pot. Add 14 cups of water. Bring to a boil. Add mushrooms if desired. Cover, lower heat and simmer for 1 hour.

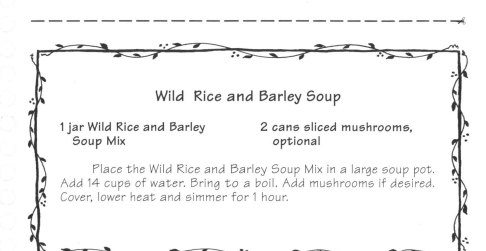

Wild Rice and Barley Soup

1 jar Wild Rice and Barley
Soup Mix

2 cans sliced mushrooms,
optional

Place the Wild Rice and Barley Soup Mix in a large soup pot. Add 14 cups of water. Bring to a boil. Add mushrooms if desired. Cover, lower heat and simmer for 1 hour.

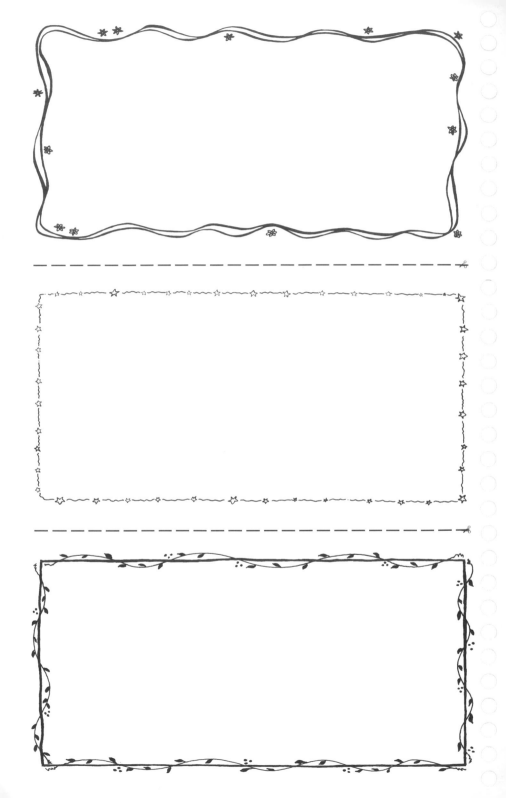

Calico Bean Soup Mix

2/3 C. yellow split peas
2/3 C. green split peas
2/3 C. dried lima beans
2/3 C. dried pinto beans
1/2 C. dry kidney beans
1/2 C. dried great Northern
   beans
1/2 C. dried minced onion
4 tsp. beef bouillon granules
1/2 tsp. ground cumin
1/2 tsp. garlic powder

Layer the ingredients in the order given into a wide-mouth 1-quart canning jar. Pack each layer in place before adding the next ingredient.

Attach a gift tag with the cooking directions.

❀ At times, it may seem impossible to make all of the jar ingredients fit, but with persistence, they do all fit. ❀

Calico Bean Soup

1 jar Calico Bean Soup Mix
4 carrots, diced
4 stalks celery, diced
4 pounds smoked ham hocks

Place the Calico Bean Soup Mix in a large soup pot. Add 16 cups of water. Bring to a boil. Cover; remove from heat and let sit for 1 hour. Return pot to heat, stir in vegetables and ham hocks. Cover, reduce heat and simmer 2 hours, until beans are tender, skimming fat as needed. Remove ham hocks from soup. Remove meat from bone, chop and return to soup. Heat through and serve.

Calico Bean Soup

1 jar Calico Bean Soup Mix 4 stalks celery, diced
4 carrots, diced 4 pounds smoked ham hocks

Place the Calico Bean Soup Mix in a large soup pot. Add 16 cups of water. Bring to a boil. Cover; remove from heat and let sit for 1 hour. Return pot to heat, stir in vegetables and ham hocks. Cover, reduce heat and simmer 2 hours, until beans are tender, skimming fat as needed. Remove ham hocks from soup. Remove meat from bone, chop and return to soup. Heat through and serve.

Calico Bean Soup

1 jar Calico Bean Soup Mix 4 stalks celery, diced
4 carrots, diced 4 pounds smoked ham hocks

Place the Calico Bean Soup Mix in a large soup pot. Add 16 cups of water. Bring to a boil. Cover; remove from heat and let sit for 1 hour. Return pot to heat, stir in vegetables and ham hocks. Cover, reduce heat and simmer 2 hours, until beans are tender, skimming fat as needed. Remove ham hocks from soup. Remove meat from bone, chop and return to soup. Heat through and serve.

Calico Bean Soup

1 jar Calico Bean Soup Mix 4 stalks celery, diced
4 carrots, diced 4 pounds smoked ham hocks

Place the Calico Bean Soup Mix in a large soup pot. Add 16 cups of water. Bring to a boil. Cover; remove from heat and let sit for 1 hour. Return pot to heat, stir in vegetables and ham hocks. Cover, reduce heat and simmer 2 hours, until beans are tender, skimming fat as needed. Remove ham hocks from soup. Remove meat from bone, chop and return to soup. Heat through and serve.

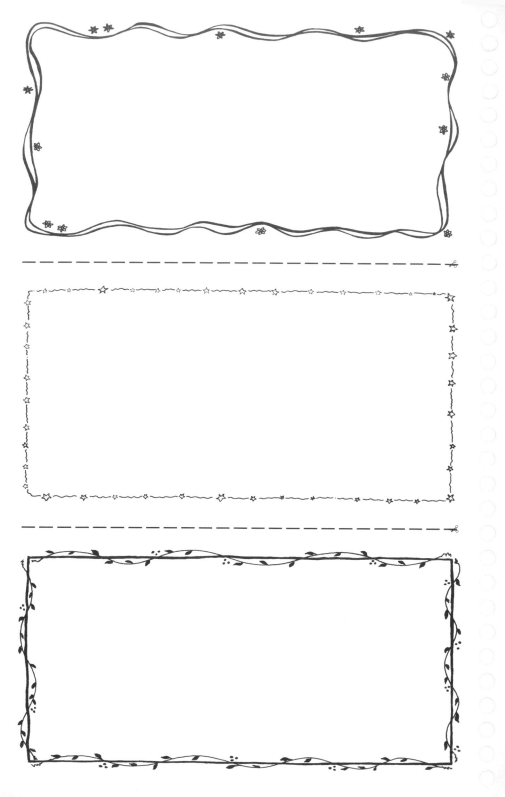

Calico Bean Soup

1 jar Calico Bean Soup Mix   4 stalks celery, diced
4 carrots, diced   4 pounds smoked ham hocks

    Place the Calico Bean Soup Mix in a large soup pot. Add 16 cups of water. Bring to a boil. Cover; remove from heat and let sit for 1 hour. Return pot to heat, stir in vegetables and ham hocks. Cover, reduce heat and simmer 2 hours, until beans are tender, skimming fat as needed. Remove ham hocks from soup. Remove meat from bone, chop and return to soup. Heat through and serve.

Calico Bean Soup

1 jar Calico Bean Soup Mix   4 stalks celery, diced
4 carrots, diced   4 pounds smoked ham hocks

    Place the Calico Bean Soup Mix in a large soup pot. Add 16 cups of water. Bring to a boil. Cover; remove from heat and let sit for 1 hour. Return pot to heat, stir in vegetables and ham hocks. Cover, reduce heat and simmer 2 hours, until beans are tender, skimming fat as needed. Remove ham hocks from soup. Remove meat from bone, chop and return to soup. Heat through and serve.

Calico Bean Soup

1 jar Calico Bean Soup Mix   4 stalks celery, diced
4 carrots, diced   4 pounds smoked ham hocks

    Place the Calico Bean Soup Mix in a large soup pot. Add 16 cups of water. Bring to a boil. Cover; remove from heat and let sit for 1 hour. Return pot to heat, stir in vegetables and ham hocks. Cover, reduce heat and simmer 2 hours, until beans are tender, skimming fat as needed. Remove ham hocks from soup. Remove meat from bone, chop and return to soup. Heat through and serve.

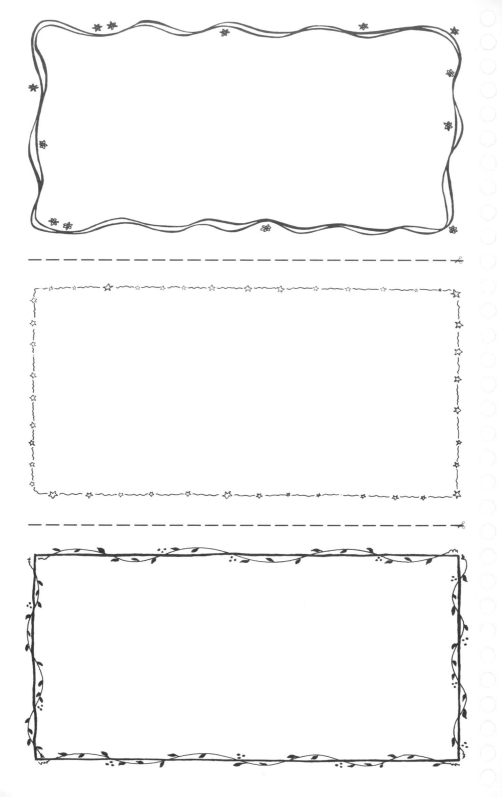

Tortilla Soup Mix

1 C. converted long grain rice
2 to 2 1/2 C. crushed tortilla
chips

Seasoning Packet:

2 T. chicken bouillon granules
2 tsp. lemonade powder with
sugar
1 tsp. lemon pepper
1 tsp. dried cilantro leaves
1/2 tsp. garlic powder
1/2 tsp. ground cumin
1/2 tsp. salt
1/4 C. dried minced onion

Place into a wide-mouth 1-quart canning jar. Mix and place the seasonings in a small plastic bag. Place the packet on top of rice. Add the crushed tortilla chips.

Attach a gift tag with the cooking directions.

Tortilla Soup

1 jar Tortilla Soup Mix
2 (5 ounce) cans chicken
1 (10 ounce) can diced
   tomatoes and green chilies

Carefully remove the tortilla chips from the Tortilla Soup Mix. Remove the seasoning packet and set aside. Place rice in a large soup pot. Add 10 cups water, chicken, tomatoes and seasoning packet. Bring to a boil. Lower heat, cover and simmer 20 minutes. Add tortilla chips. Cover and simmer 5 more minutes. Serve immediately.

Tortilla Soup

1 jar Tortilla Soup Mix
2 (5 ounce) cans chicken

1 (10 ounce) can diced
tomatoes and green chilies

   Carefully remove the tortilla chips from the Tortilla Soup Mix. Remove the seasoning packet and set aside. Place rice in a large soup pot. Add 10 cups water, chicken, tomatoes and seasoning packet. Bring to a boil. Lower heat, cover and simmer 20 minutes. Add tortilla chips. Cover and simmer 5 more minutes. Serve immediately.

Tortilla Soup

1 jar Tortilla Soup Mix
2 (5 ounce) cans chicken

1 (10 ounce) can diced
tomatoes and green chilies

   Carefully remove the tortilla chips from the Tortilla Soup Mix. Remove the seasoning packet and set aside. Place rice in a large soup pot. Add 10 cups water, chicken, tomatoes and seasoning packet. Bring to a boil. Lower heat, cover and simmer 20 minutes. Add tortilla chips. Cover and simmer 5 more minutes. Serve immediately.

Tortilla Soup

1 jar Tortilla Soup Mix
2 (5 ounce) cans chicken

1 (10 ounce) can diced
tomatoes and green chilies

   Carefully remove the tortilla chips from the Tortilla Soup Mix. Remove the seasoning packet and set aside. Place rice in a large soup pot. Add 10 cups water, chicken, tomatoes and seasoning packet. Bring to a boil. Lower heat, cover and simmer 20 minutes. Add tortilla chips. Cover and simmer 5 more minutes. Serve immediately.

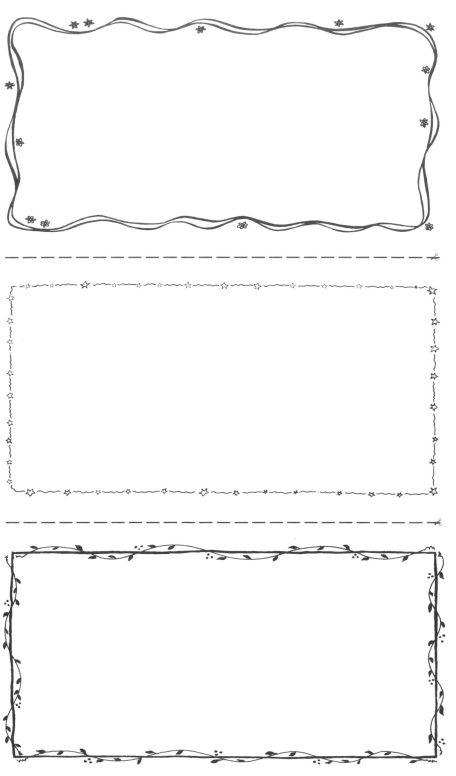

Tortilla Soup

1 jar Tortilla Soup Mix
2 (5 ounce) cans chicken

1 (10 ounce) can diced
tomatoes and green chilies

Carefully remove the tortilla chips from the Tortilla Soup Mix. Remove the seasoning packet and set aside. Place rice in a large soup pot. Add 10 cups water, chicken, tomatoes and seasoning packet. Bring to a boil. Lower heat, cover and simmer 20 minutes. Add tortilla chips. Cover and simmer 5 more minutes. Serve immediately.

Tortilla Soup

1 jar Tortilla Soup Mix
2 (5 ounce) cans chicken

1 (10 ounce) can diced
tomatoes and green chilies

Carefully remove the tortilla chips from the Tortilla Soup Mix. Remove the seasoning packet and set aside. Place rice in a large soup pot. Add 10 cups water, chicken, tomatoes and seasoning packet. Bring to a boil. Lower heat, cover and simmer 20 minutes. Add tortilla chips. Cover and simmer 5 more minutes. Serve immediately.

Tortilla Soup

1 jar Tortilla Soup Mix
2 (5 ounce) cans chicken

1 (10 ounce) can diced
tomatoes and green chilies

Carefully remove the tortilla chips from the Tortilla Soup Mix. Remove the seasoning packet and set aside. Place rice in a large soup pot. Add 10 cups water, chicken, tomatoes and seasoning packet. Bring to a boil. Lower heat, cover and simmer 20 minutes. Add tortilla chips. Cover and simmer 5 more minutes. Serve immediately.

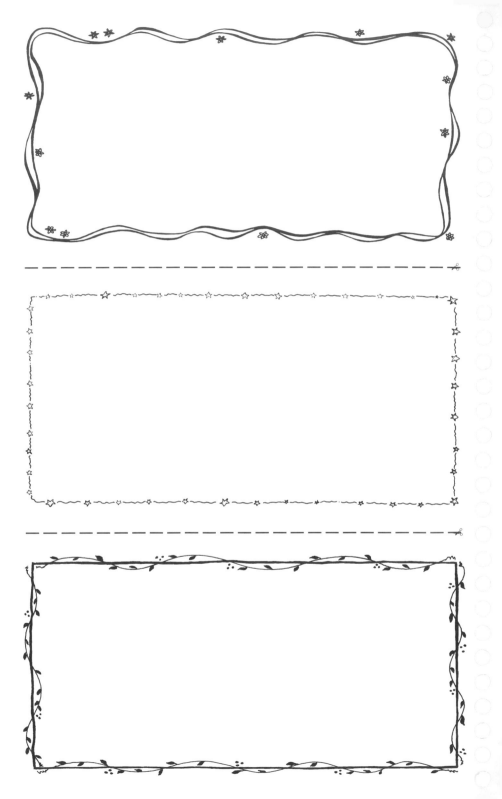

Black Bean Soup Mix

Seasoning Packet:
- 1/4 C. dried minced onion
- 2 (0.87 ounce) packages brown gravy mix
- 2 (1.25 ounce) packages chili seasoning
- 1/2 C. dried parsley flakes

2 1/2 C. dried black beans

Layer the ingredients in the order given into a wide-mouth 1-quart canning jar. Mix and place the seasonings in a small plastic bag. Place the packet in the bottom of the jar and fill with beans.

Attach a gift tag with the cooking directions.

Black Bean Soup

1 jar Black Bean Soup Mix
2 (10 ounce) cans diced
   tomatoes and green chilies

Remove beans from Black Bean Soup Mix. Set aside seasoning packet. Rinse beans and place in microwave safe dish. Cover with water, 1 to 2 inches over top of beans. Soak beans in water at least 12 hours or cover dish loosely with plastic wrap and microwave on high for 20 minutes, rotating after 10 minutes. Drain and rinse beans very well. Place beans in a large soup pot. Add 10 cups water and seasoning packet. Cover, bring to a boil. Lower heat, cover and simmer for 1 1/2 hours. Add tomatoes and simmer for an additional 1/2 hour or until beans are firm but tender.

Black Bean Soup

1 jar Black Bean Soup Mix

2 (10 ounce) cans diced tomatoes and green chilies

Remove beans from Black Bean Soup Mix. Set aside seasoning packet. Rinse beans and place in microwave safe dish. Cover with water, 1 to 2 inches over top of beans. Soak beans in water at least 12 hours or cover dish loosely with plastic wrap and microwave on high for 20 minutes, rotating after 10 minutes. Drain and rinse beans very well. Place beans in a large soup pot. Add 10 cups water and seasoning packet. Cover, bring to a boil. Lower heat, cover and simmer for 1 1/2 hours. Add tomatoes and simmer for an additional 1/2 hour or until beans are firm but tender.

Black Bean Soup

1 jar Black Bean Soup Mix

2 (10 ounce) cans diced tomatoes and green chilies

Remove beans from Black Bean Soup Mix. Set aside seasoning packet. Rinse beans and place in microwave safe dish. Cover with water, 1 to 2 inches over top of beans. Soak beans in water at least 12 hours or cover dish loosely with plastic wrap and microwave on high for 20 minutes, rotating after 10 minutes. Drain and rinse beans very well. Place beans in a large soup pot. Add 10 cups water and seasoning packet. Cover, bring to a boil. Lower heat, cover and simmer for 1 1/2 hours. Add tomatoes and simmer for an additional 1/2 hour or until beans are firm but tender.

Black Bean Soup

1 jar Black Bean Soup Mix

2 (10 ounce) cans diced tomatoes and green chilies

Remove beans from Black Bean Soup Mix. Set aside seasoning packet. Rinse beans and place in microwave safe dish. Cover with water, 1 to 2 inches over top of beans. Soak beans in water at least 12 hours or cover dish loosely with plastic wrap and microwave on high for 20 minutes, rotating after 10 minutes. Drain and rinse beans very well. Place beans in a large soup pot. Add 10 cups water and seasoning packet. Cover, bring to a boil. Lower heat, cover and simmer for 1 1/2 hours. Add tomatoes and simmer for an additional 1/2 hour or until beans are firm but tender.

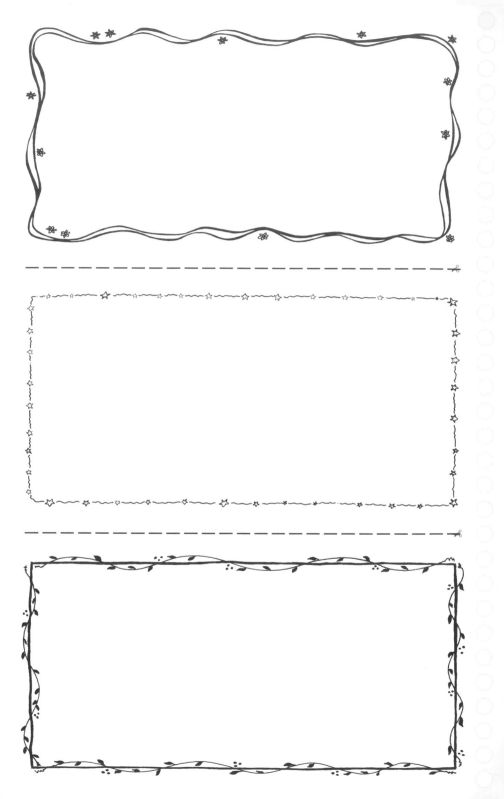

Black Bean Soup

1 jar Black Bean Soup Mix

2 (10 ounce) cans diced tomatoes and green chilies

Remove beans from Black Bean Soup Mix. Set aside seasoning packet. Rinse beans and place in microwave safe dish. Cover with water, 1 to 2 inches over top of beans. Soak beans in water at least 12 hours or cover dish loosely with plastic wrap and microwave on high for 20 minutes, rotating after 10 minutes. Drain and rinse beans very well. Place beans in a large soup pot. Add 10 cups water and seasoning packet. Cover, bring to a boil. Lower heat, cover and simmer for 1 1/2 hours. Add tomatoes and simmer for an additional 1/2 hour or until beans are firm but tender.

Black Bean Soup

1 jar Black Bean Soup Mix

2 (10 ounce) cans diced tomatoes and green chilies

Remove beans from Black Bean Soup Mix. Set aside seasoning packet. Rinse beans and place in microwave safe dish. Cover with water, 1 to 2 inches over top of beans. Soak beans in water at least 12 hours or cover dish loosely with plastic wrap and microwave on high for 20 minutes, rotating after 10 minutes. Drain and rinse beans very well. Place beans in a large soup pot. Add 10 cups water and seasoning packet. Cover, bring to a boil. Lower heat, cover and simmer for 1 1/2 hours. Add tomatoes and simmer for an additional 1/2 hour or until beans are firm but tender.

Black Bean Soup

1 jar Black Bean Soup Mix

2 (10 ounce) cans diced tomatoes and green chilies

Remove beans from Black Bean Soup Mix. Set aside seasoning packet. Rinse beans and place in microwave safe dish. Cover with water, 1 to 2 inches over top of beans. Soak beans in water at least 12 hours or cover dish loosely with plastic wrap and microwave on high for 20 minutes, rotating after 10 minutes. Drain and rinse beans very well. Place beans in a large soup pot. Add 10 cups water and seasoning packet. Cover, bring to a boil. Lower heat, cover and simmer for 1 1/2 hours. Add tomatoes and simmer for an additional 1/2 hour or until beans are firm but tender.

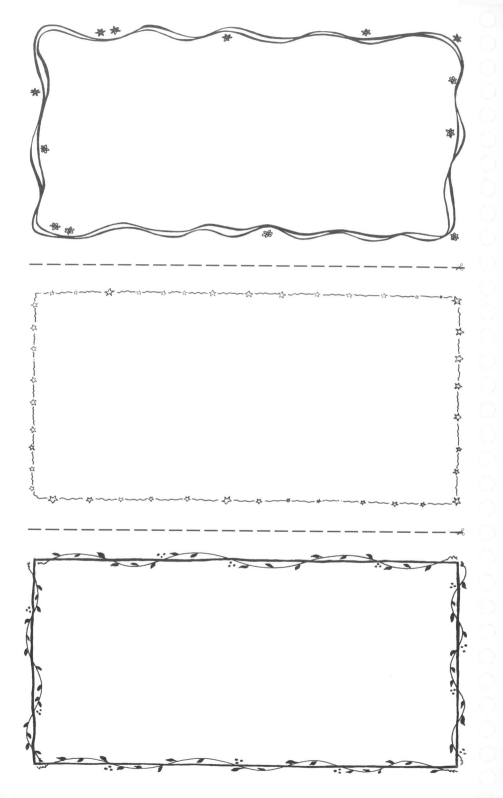

Cream of Onion Soup Mix

1 1/2 C. whole wheat
   pastry flour
1 1/4 C. instant
   powdered milk
2/3 C. dried onion
2 tsp. pepper
1 tsp. garlic powder
1/3 C. dried parsley
1 tsp. salt
1/3 C. chicken bouillion
   granules

In a bowl, combine all ingredients and mix thoroughly. Place into a wide-mouth 1-quart canning jar.

Attach a gift tag with the cooking directions.

Cream of Onion Soup

1 jar Cream of Onion Soup Mix
16 C. milk

Place the Cream of Onion Soup Mix in a large soup pot. Add milk. Mix well and bring to a boil. Boil 4 to 6 minutes, stirring constantly and scraping bottom of pan. Use 1/4 cup Cream of Onion Soup Mix plus 1 cup milk for an individual serving.

Cream of Onion Soup

1 jar Cream of Onion Soup Mix   16 C. milk

Place the Cream of Onion Soup Mix in a large soup pot. Add milk. Mix well and bring to a boil. Boil 4 to 6 minutes, stirring constantly and scraping bottom of pan. Use 1/4 cup Cream of Onion Soup Mix plus 1 cup milk for an individual serving.

Cream of Onion Soup

1 jar Cream of Onion Soup Mix   16 C. milk

Place the Cream of Onion Soup Mix in a large soup pot. Add milk. Mix well and bring to a boil. Boil 4 to 6 minutes, stirring constantly and scraping bottom of pan. Use 1/4 cup Cream of Onion Soup Mix plus 1 cup milk for an individual serving.

Cream of Onion Soup

1 jar Cream of Onion Soup Mix   16 C. milk

Place the Cream of Onion Soup Mix in a large soup pot. Add milk. Mix well and bring to a boil. Boil 4 to 6 minutes, stirring constantly and scraping bottom of pan. Use 1/4 cup Cream of Onion Soup Mix plus 1 cup milk for an individual serving.

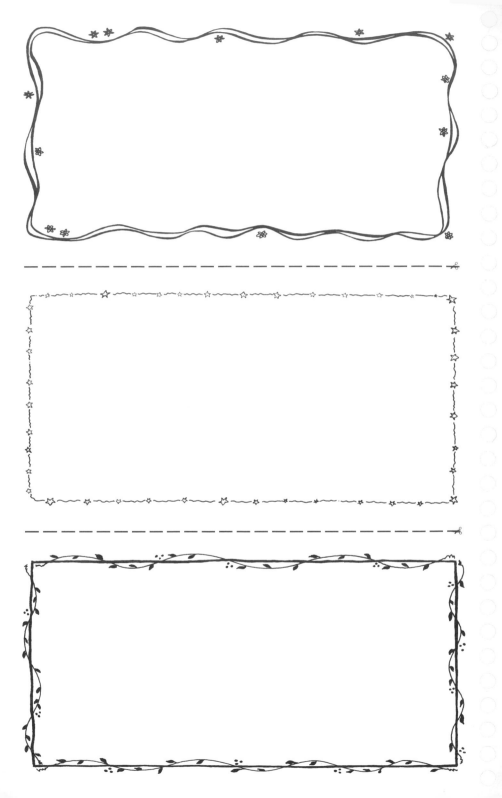

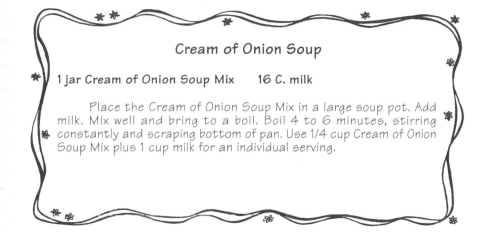

Cream of Onion Soup

1 jar Cream of Onion Soup Mix   16 C. milk

Place the Cream of Onion Soup Mix in a large soup pot. Add milk. Mix well and bring to a boil. Boil 4 to 6 minutes, stirring constantly and scraping bottom of pan. Use 1/4 cup Cream of Onion Soup Mix plus 1 cup milk for an individual serving.

Cream of Onion Soup

1 jar Cream of Onion Soup Mix   16 C. milk

Place the Cream of Onion Soup Mix in a large soup pot. Add milk. Mix well and bring to a boil. Boil 4 to 6 minutes, stirring constantly and scraping bottom of pan. Use 1/4 cup Cream of Onion Soup Mix plus 1 cup milk for an individual serving.

Cream of Onion Soup

1 jar Cream of Onion Soup Mix   16 C. milk

Place the Cream of Onion Soup Mix in a large soup pot. Add milk. Mix well and bring to a boil. Boil 4 to 6 minutes, stirring constantly and scraping bottom of pan. Use 1/4 cup Cream of Onion Soup Mix plus 1 cup milk for an individual serving.

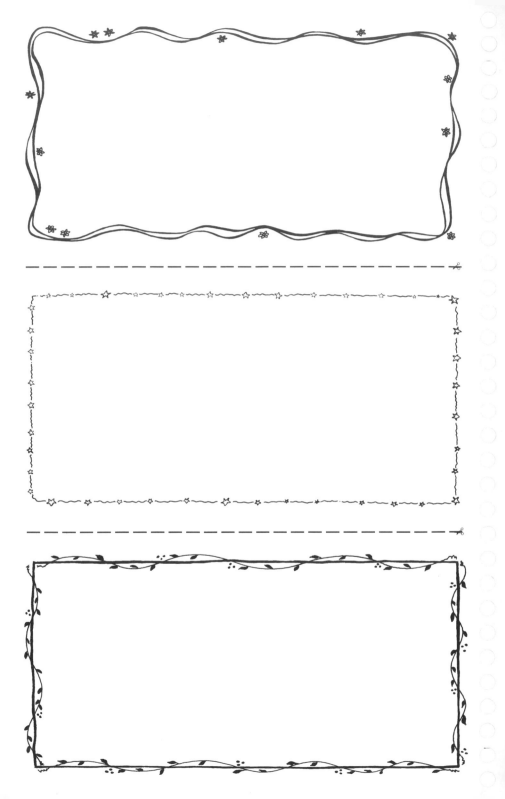

Split Pea Soup Mix

1 1/2 C. dried split peas
1/2 C. Hungry Jack® instant
   potato flakes
1/4 C. dried minced onion
2 tsp. chicken bouillon granules
2 tsp. powdered lemonade mix
with sugar
1 tsp. dried minced garlic
1 tsp. salt
2 T. dried parsley flakes
2 tsp. dried thyme leaves
1 tsp. celery flakes
1/2 C. Hungry Jack® instant
   potato flakes
1 1/2 C. dried split peas

Layer the ingredients in the order given into a wide-mouth 1-quart canning jar. Pack each layer in place before adding the next ingredient.

Attach a gift tag with the cooking directions.

Split Pea Soup

1 jar Split Pea Soup Mix
2 (5 ounce) cans ham, optional

Place the Split Pea Soup Mix in a large soup pot. Add 10 cups of water. Bring to a boil. Lower heat and simmer for 1 1/2 hours, stirring occasionally. Puree soup in blender. Heat ham in microwave and stir in after pureeing soup.

Split Pea Soup

1 jar Split Pea Soup Mix   2 (5 ounce) cans ham,
optional

Place the Split Pea Soup Mix in a large soup pot. Add 10 cups of water. Bring to a boil. Lower heat and simmer for 1 1/2 hours, stirring occasionally. Puree soup in blender. Heat ham in microwave and stir in after pureeing soup.

Split Pea Soup

1 jar Split Pea Soup Mix   2 (5 ounce) cans ham,
optional

Place the Split Pea Soup Mix in a large soup pot. Add 10 cups of water. Bring to a boil. Lower heat and simmer for 1 1/2 hours, stirring occasionally. Puree soup in blender. Heat ham in microwave and stir in after pureeing soup.

Split Pea Soup

1 jar Split Pea Soup Mix   2 (5 ounce) cans ham,
optional

Place the Split Pea Soup Mix in a large soup pot. Add 10 cups of water. Bring to a boil. Lower heat and simmer for 1 1/2 hours, stirring occasionally. Puree soup in blender. Heat ham in microwave and stir in after pureeing soup.

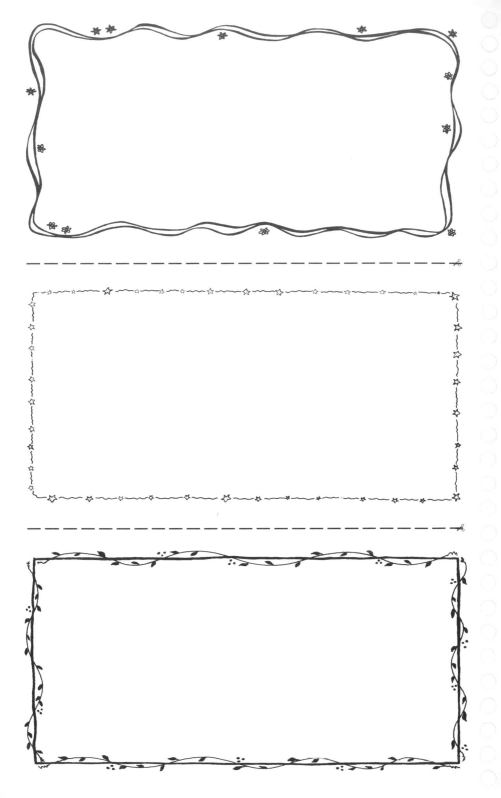

Split Pea Soup

1 jar Split Pea Soup Mix

2 (5 ounce) cans ham, optional

Place the Split Pea Soup Mix in a large soup pot. Add 10 cups of water. Bring to a boil. Lower heat and simmer for 1 1/2 hours, stirring occasionally. Puree soup in blender. Heat ham in microwave and stir in after pureeing soup.

Split Pea Soup

1 jar Split Pea Soup Mix

2 (5 ounce) cans ham, optional

Place the Split Pea Soup Mix in a large soup pot. Add 10 cups of water. Bring to a boil. Lower heat and simmer for 1 1/2 hours, stirring occasionally. Puree soup in blender. Heat ham in microwave and stir in after pureeing soup.

Split Pea Soup

1 jar Split Pea Soup Mix

2 (5 ounce) cans ham, optional

Place the Split Pea Soup Mix in a large soup pot. Add 10 cups of water. Bring to a boil. Lower heat and simmer for 1 1/2 hours, stirring occasionally. Puree soup in blender. Heat ham in microwave and stir in after pureeing soup.

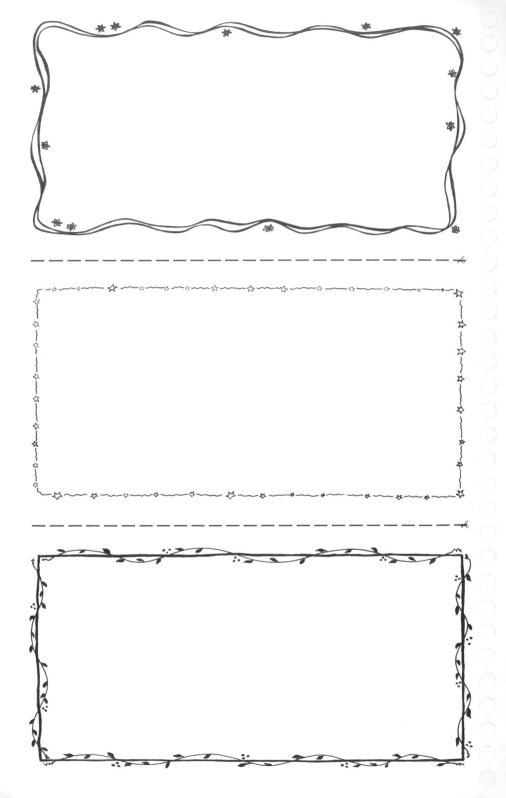

Creamy Cheese Soup Mix

1 (1.5 ounce) package Knorr® Four Cheese Sauce Mix
3 tsp. chicken bouillon granules
1/2 tsp. pepper
1 (1.4 ounce) package Knorr® Vegetable Soup Mix
1/4 C. dried parsley flakes
3 C. powdered coffee creamer
1/4 C. cornstarch

Layer the ingredients in the order given into a wide-mouth 1-quart canning jar. Pack each layer in place before adding the next ingredient.

Attach a gift tag with the cooking directions.

❀ *For a great gift, fill a large soup pot with jar mixes, pot holders, kitchen towels, cookbooks, recipe cards, and a ladle.* ❀

Creamy Cheese Soup

1 jar Creamy Cheese Soup Mix

Place the Creamy Cheese Soup Mix in a large soup pot. Add 5 cups boiling water. Mix well and bring to a boil. Boil 4 to 6 minutes, stirring often and scraping bottom of pan.

Creamy Cheese Soup

1 jar Creamy Cheese Soup Mix

Place the Creamy Cheese Soup Mix in a large soup pot. Add 5 cups boiling water. Mix well and bring to a boil. Boil 4 to 6 minutes, stirring often and scraping bottom of pan.

Creamy Cheese Soup

1 jar Creamy Cheese Soup Mix

Place the Creamy Cheese Soup Mix in a large soup pot. Add 5 cups boiling water. Mix well and bring to a boil. Boil 4 to 6 minutes, stirring often and scraping bottom of pan.

Creamy Cheese Soup

1 jar Creamy Cheese Soup Mix

Place the Creamy Cheese Soup Mix in a large soup pot. Add 5 cups boiling water. Mix well and bring to a boil. Boil 4 to 6 minutes, stirring often and scraping bottom of pan.

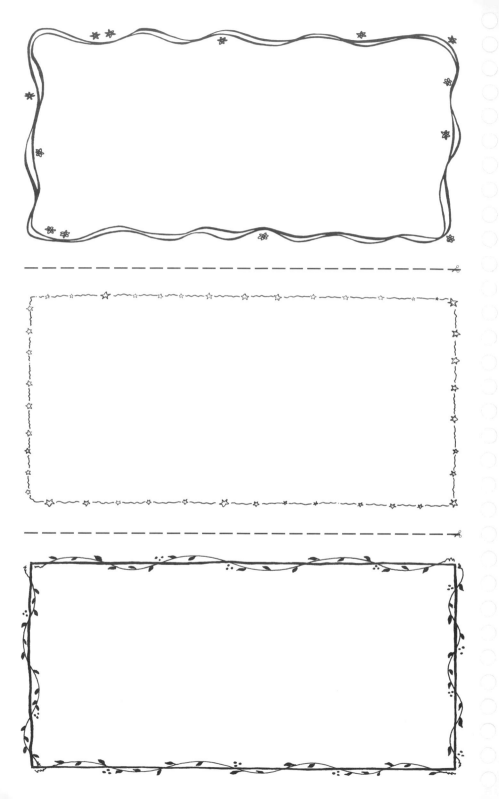

Creamy Cheese Soup

1 jar Creamy Cheese Soup Mix

Place the Creamy Cheese Soup Mix in a large soup pot. Add 5 cups boiling water. Mix well and bring to a boil. Boil 4 to 6 minutes, stirring often and scraping bottom of pan.

Creamy Cheese Soup

1 jar Creamy Cheese Soup Mix

Place the Creamy Cheese Soup Mix in a large soup pot. Add 5 cups boiling water. Mix well and bring to a boil. Boil 4 to 6 minutes, stirring often and scraping bottom of pan.

Creamy Cheese Soup

1 jar Creamy Cheese Soup Mix

Place the Creamy Cheese Soup Mix in a large soup pot. Add 5 cups boiling water. Mix well and bring to a boil. Boil 4 to 6 minutes, stirring often and scraping bottom of pan.

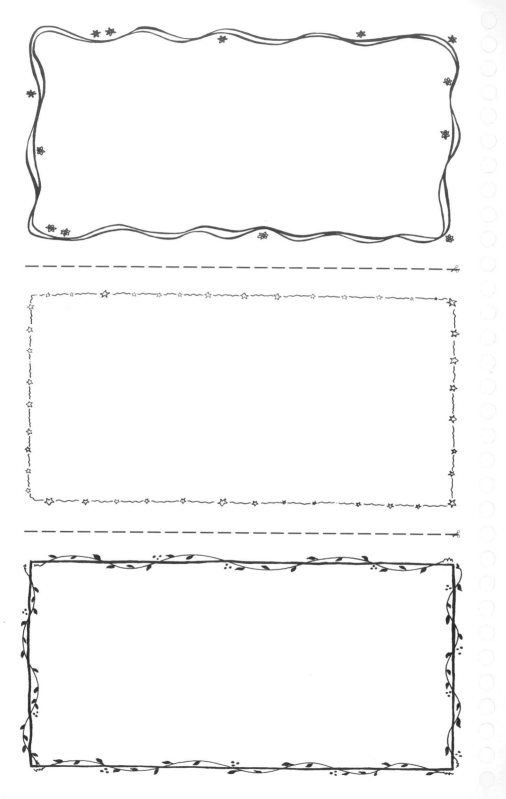

Patchwork Soup Mix

1 C. barley
1 C. dried split peas
1 C. uncooked white rice
3/4 C. dry lentils
2 T. dried parsley
2 tsp. granulated garlic
1 tsp. pepper
2 tsp. salt
1 tsp. garlic powder
2 tsp. Italian seasoning
2 tsp. dried sage

Layer the ingredients in the order given into a wide-mouth 1-quart canning jar. Pack each layer in place before adding the next ingredient.

Attach a gift tag with the cooking directions.

Patchwork Soup

1 jar Patchwork Soup Mix
1 chopped medium onion

Place the Patchwork Soup Mix in a large soup pot. Add 20 cups of water. Add onion. Bring to a boil. Cover, lower heat and simmer for 1 hour, stirring occasionally. Check after 30 minutes and add additional water if necessary.

Patchwork Soup

1 jar Patchwork Soup Mix   1 chopped medium onion

Place the Patchwork Soup Mix in a large soup pot. Add 20 cups of water. Add onion. Bring to a boil. Cover, lower heat and simmer for 1 hour, stirring occasionally. Check after 30 minutes and add additional water if necessary.

Patchwork Soup

1 jar Patchwork Soup Mix   1 chopped medium onion

Place the Patchwork Soup Mix in a large soup pot. Add 20 cups of water. Add onion. Bring to a boil. Cover, lower heat and simmer for 1 hour, stirring occasionally. Check after 30 minutes and add additional water if necessary.

Patchwork Soup

1 jar Patchwork Soup Mix   1 chopped medium onion

Place the Patchwork Soup Mix in a large soup pot. Add 20 cups of water. Add onion. Bring to a boil. Cover, lower heat and simmer for 1 hour, stirring occasionally. Check after 30 minutes and add additional water if necessary.

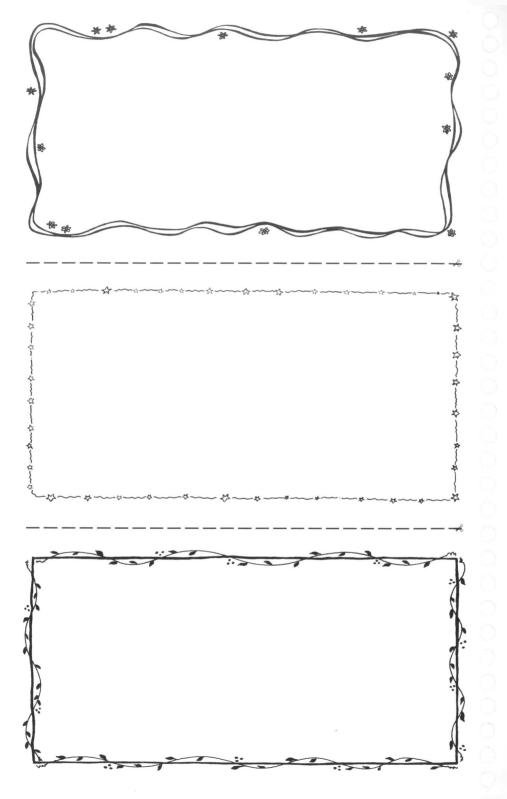

Patchwork Soup

1 jar Patchwork Soup Mix   1 chopped medium onion

Place the Patchwork Soup Mix in a large soup pot. Add 20 cups of water. Add onion. Bring to a boil. Cover, lower heat and simmer for 1 hour, stirring occasionally. Check after 30 minutes and add additional water if necessary.

Patchwork Soup

1 jar Patchwork Soup Mix   1 chopped medium onion

Place the Patchwork Soup Mix in a large soup pot. Add 20 cups of water. Add onion. Bring to a boil. Cover, lower heat and simmer for 1 hour, stirring occasionally. Check after 30 minutes and add additional water if necessary.

Patchwork Soup

1 jar Patchwork Soup Mix   1 chopped medium onion

Place the Patchwork Soup Mix in a large soup pot. Add 20 cups of water. Add onion. Bring to a boil. Cover, lower heat and simmer for 1 hour, stirring occasionally. Check after 30 minutes and add additional water if necessary.

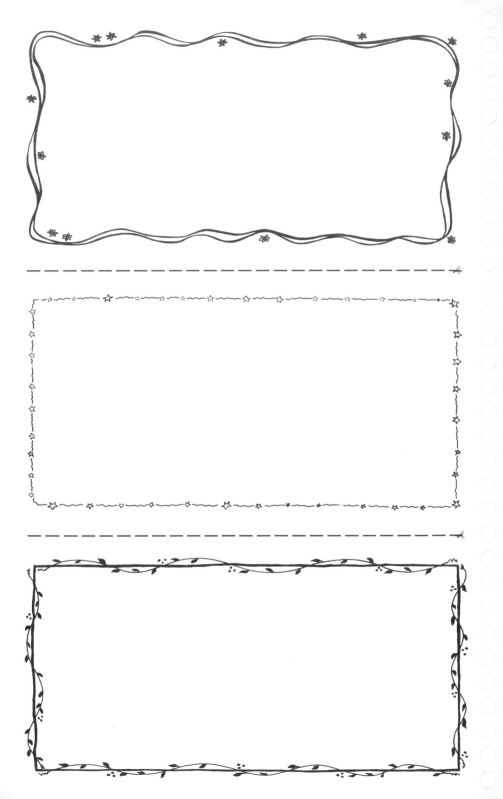

Cream of Mushroom
Soup Mix

2 C. whole wheat pastry flour
1 C. instant powdered
   milk
3/4 C. dried mushrooms
3 T. dried onion
3 T. dried parsley
1 tsp. dried minced garlic
1 tsp. salt

In a bowl, combine all ingredients and mix thoroughly. Place into a wide-mouth 1-quart canning jar.

Attach a gift tag with the cooking directions.

Cream of Mushroom Soup

1 jar Cream of Mushroom
    Soup Mix
16 C. milk
1/4 C. butter or margarine

Place the Cream of Mushroom Soup Mix in a large soup pot. Add milk and butter. Mix well and bring to a boil. Boil 4 to 6 minutes, stirring constantly and scraping bottom of pan. Use 1/4 cup Cream of Mushroom Soup Mix plus 1 cup milk for an individual serving.

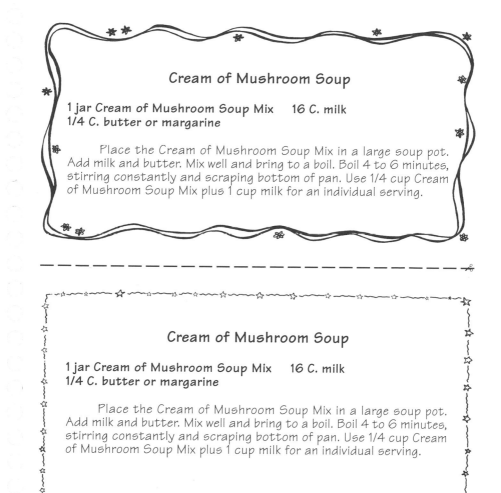

Cream of Mushroom Soup

1 jar Cream of Mushroom Soup Mix   16 C. milk
1/4 C. butter or margarine

Place the Cream of Mushroom Soup Mix in a large soup pot. Add milk and butter. Mix well and bring to a boil. Boil 4 to 6 minutes, stirring constantly and scraping bottom of pan. Use 1/4 cup Cream of Mushroom Soup Mix plus 1 cup milk for an individual serving.

Cream of Mushroom Soup

1 jar Cream of Mushroom Soup Mix   16 C. milk
1/4 C. butter or margarine

Place the Cream of Mushroom Soup Mix in a large soup pot. Add milk and butter. Mix well and bring to a boil. Boil 4 to 6 minutes, stirring constantly and scraping bottom of pan. Use 1/4 cup Cream of Mushroom Soup Mix plus 1 cup milk for an individual serving.

Cream of Mushroom Soup

1 jar Cream of Mushroom Soup Mix   16 C. milk
1/4 C. butter or margarine

Place the Cream of Mushroom Soup Mix in a large soup pot. Add milk and butter. Mix well and bring to a boil. Boil 4 to 6 minutes, stirring constantly and scraping bottom of pan. Use 1/4 cup Cream of Mushroom Soup Mix plus 1 cup milk for an individual serving.

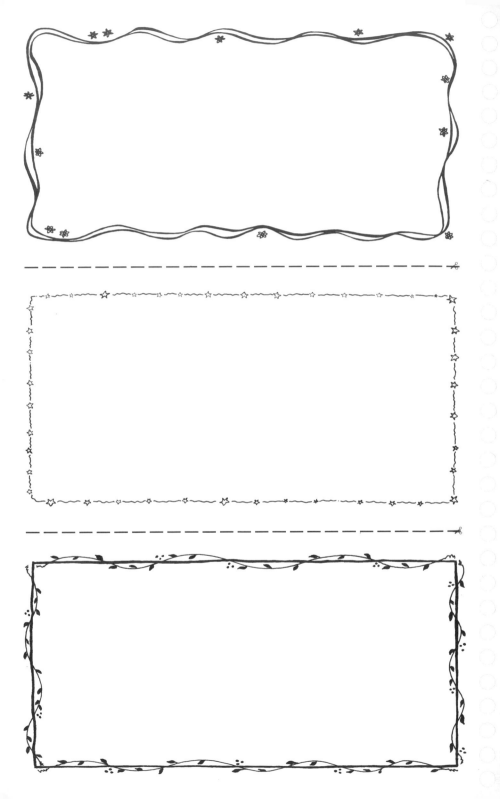

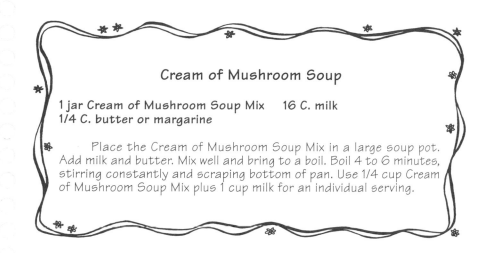

Cream of Mushroom Soup

1 jar Cream of Mushroom Soup Mix   16 C. milk
1/4 C. butter or margarine

   Place the Cream of Mushroom Soup Mix in a large soup pot. Add milk and butter. Mix well and bring to a boil. Boil 4 to 6 minutes, stirring constantly and scraping bottom of pan. Use 1/4 cup Cream of Mushroom Soup Mix plus 1 cup milk for an individual serving.

Cream of Mushroom Soup

1 jar Cream of Mushroom Soup Mix   16 C. milk
1/4 C. butter or margarine

   Place the Cream of Mushroom Soup Mix in a large soup pot. Add milk and butter. Mix well and bring to a boil. Boil 4 to 6 minutes, stirring constantly and scraping bottom of pan. Use 1/4 cup Cream of Mushroom Soup Mix plus 1 cup milk for an individual serving.

Cream of Mushroom Soup

1 jar Cream of Mushroom Soup Mix   16 C. milk
1/4 C. butter or margarine

   Place the Cream of Mushroom Soup Mix in a large soup pot. Add milk and butter. Mix well and bring to a boil. Boil 4 to 6 minutes, stirring constantly and scraping bottom of pan. Use 1/4 cup Cream of Mushroom Soup Mix plus 1 cup milk for an individual serving.

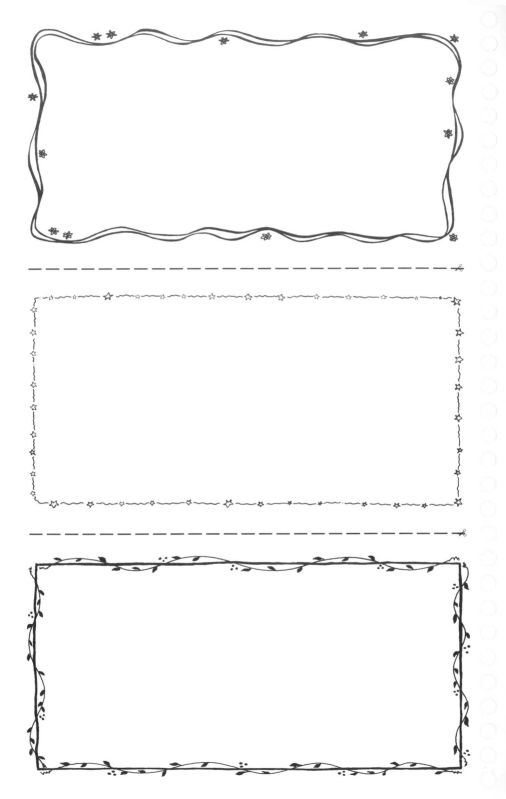

Cheesy Potato Soup Mix

2 C. powdered coffee creamer
1/2 C. imitation bacon bits
2 (1.5 ounce) packages Knorr®
  Four Cheese Sauce Mix
2 T. dried parsley flakes
1 tsp. salt-free seasoning
  blend
1 tsp. dried minced onion
1/2 tsp. pepper
2 C. Hungry Jack® potato
  flakes

Layer the ingredients in the order given into a wide-mouth 1-quart canning jar. Pack each layer in place before adding the next ingredient.

Attach a gift tag with the cooking directions.

Cheesy Potato Soup

1 jar Cheesy Potato Soup Mix
2 (5 ounce) cans ham, optional

Place the Cheesy Potato Soup Mix in a large soup pot. Add 8 cups boiling water. Mix well and let stand 5 minutes. Heat ham in microwave and stir in.

Cheesy Potato Soup

1 jar Cheesy Potato Soup Mix

2 (5 ounce) cans ham, optional

Place the Cheesy Potato Soup Mix in a large soup pot. Add 8 cups boiling water. Mix well and let stand 5 minutes. Heat ham in microwave and stir in.

Cheesy Potato Soup

1 jar Cheesy Potato Soup Mix

2 (5 ounce) cans ham, optional

Place the Cheesy Potato Soup Mix in a large soup pot. Add 8 cups boiling water. Mix well and let stand 5 minutes. Heat ham in microwave and stir in.

Cheesy Potato Soup

1 jar Cheesy Potato Soup Mix

2 (5 ounce) cans ham, optional

Place the Cheesy Potato Soup Mix in a large soup pot. Add 8 cups boiling water. Mix well and let stand 5 minutes. Heat ham in microwave and stir in.

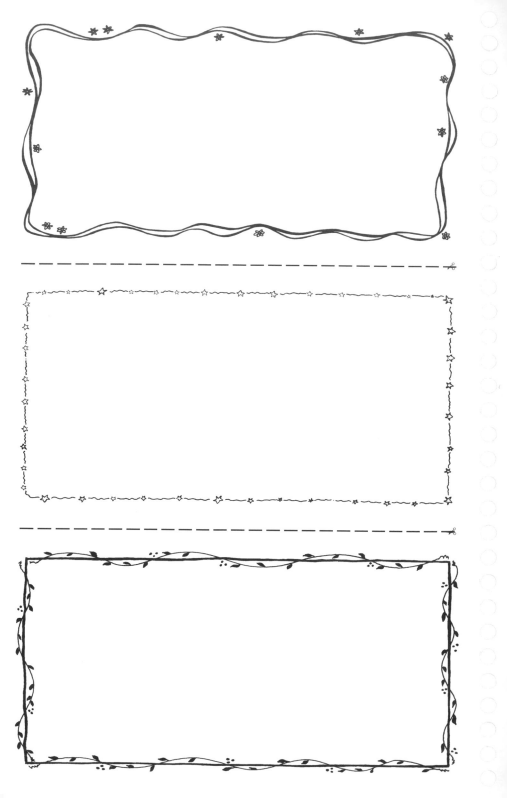

Cheesy Potato Soup

1 jar Cheesy Potato Soup Mix   2 (5 ounce) cans ham, optional

Place the Cheesy Potato Soup Mix in a large soup pot. Add 8 cups boiling water. Mix well and let stand 5 minutes. Heat ham in microwave and stir in.

Cheesy Potato Soup

1 jar Cheesy Potato Soup Mix   2 (5 ounce) cans ham, optional

Place the Cheesy Potato Soup Mix in a large soup pot. Add 8 cups boiling water. Mix well and let stand 5 minutes. Heat ham in microwave and stir in.

Cheesy Potato Soup

1 jar Cheesy Potato Soup Mix   2 (5 ounce) cans ham, optional

Place the Cheesy Potato Soup Mix in a large soup pot. Add 8 cups boiling water. Mix well and let stand 5 minutes. Heat ham in microwave and stir in.

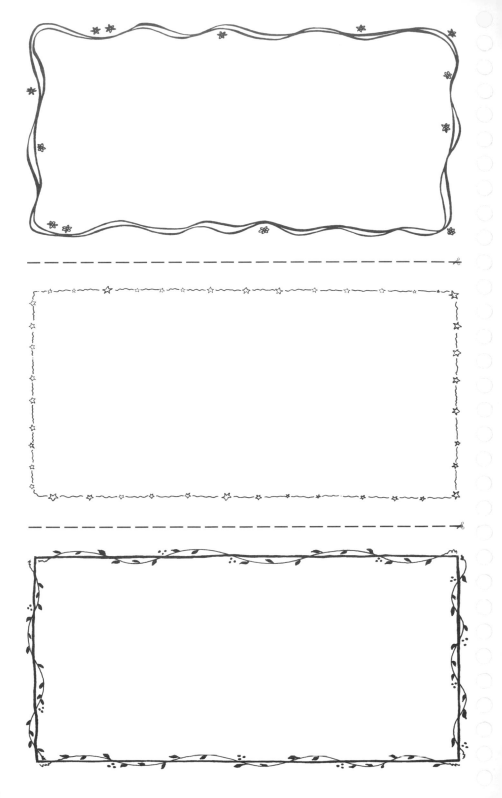

Potato Soup Mix

1 1/2 C. Hungry Jack® instant
potato flakes
1/2 C. powdered coffee
creamer
1 (1 ounce) package chicken
gravy mix
2 T. dried parsley flakes
1/4 C. grated Parmesan
cheese
2 tsp. seasoning blend
1 tsp. dried minced onion
1/2 tsp. pepper
1 1/2 C. Hungry Jack® instant
potato flakes
1/2 C. powdered coffee
creamer

Layer the ingredients in the order given
into a wide-mouth 1-quart canning jar. Pack
each layer in place before adding the next
ingredient.

Attach a gift tag with the cooking
directions.

Potato Soup

1 jar Potato Soup Mix

Place the Potato Soup Mix in a large soup pot. Add 8 cups boiling water. Mix well and let stand 5 minutes to thicken. Serve immediately.

Potato Soup

1 jar Potato Soup Mix

Place the Potato Soup Mix in a large soup pot. Add 8 cups boiling water. Mix well and let stand 5 minutes to thicken. Serve immediately.

Potato Soup

1 jar Potato Soup Mix

Place the Potato Soup Mix in a large soup pot. Add 8 cups boiling water. Mix well and let stand 5 minutes to thicken. Serve immediately.

Potato Soup

1 jar Potato Soup Mix

Place the Potato Soup Mix in a large soup pot. Add 8 cups boiling water. Mix well and let stand 5 minutes to thicken. Serve immediately.

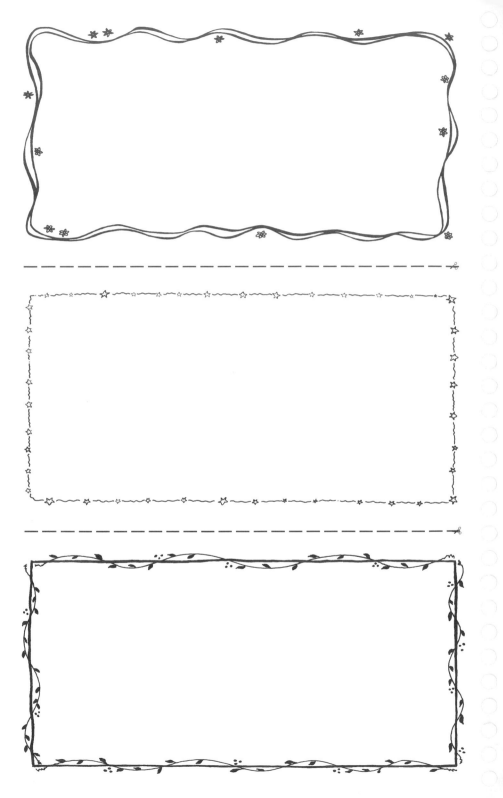

Potato Soup

1 jar Potato Soup Mix

Place the Potato Soup Mix in a large soup pot. Add 8 cups boiling water. Mix well and let stand 5 minutes to thicken. Serve immediately.

Potato Soup

1 jar Potato Soup Mix

Place the Potato Soup Mix in a large soup pot. Add 8 cups boiling water. Mix well and let stand 5 minutes to thicken. Serve immediately.

Potato Soup

1 jar Potato Soup Mix

Place the Potato Soup Mix in a large soup pot. Add 8 cups boiling water. Mix well and let stand 5 minutes to thicken. Serve immediately.

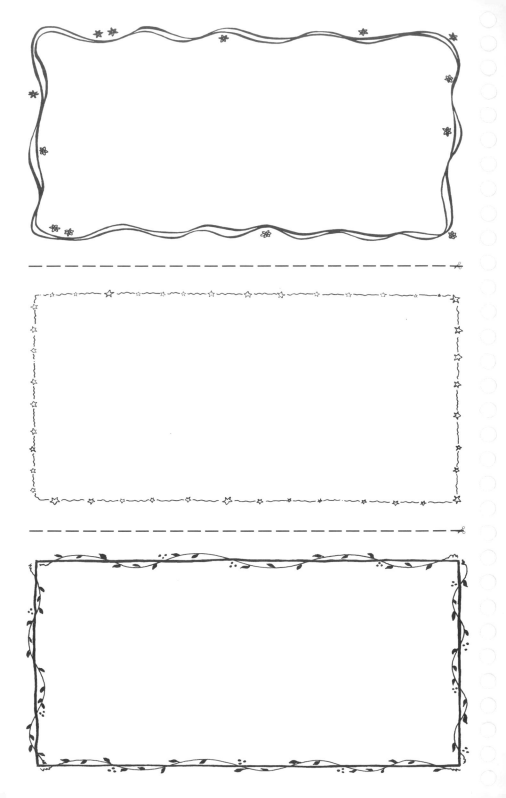

Lentil Soup Mix

4 C. dried lentils
6 chicken bouillon cubes,
crumbled
1 tsp. dried thyme
1 tsp. garlic powder

Layer the ingredients in the order given into a wide-mouth 1-quart canning jar. Pack each layer in place before adding the next ingredient.

Attach a gift tag with the cooking directions.

❀ Small appliques or embroidery can be added to the center of a fabric cover to further personalize the gift. ❀

Lentil Soup

1 jar Lentil Soup Mix
4 carrots, diced
4 stalks celery, diced
1 C. chopped onion

Place the Lentil Soup Mix in a large soup pot. Add 9 cups water and bring to a boil. Add the vegetables and simmer the soup partially covered for 2 hours or until the lentils are soft.

Lentil Soup

1 jar Lentil Soup Mix
4 carrots, diced

4 stalks celery, diced
1 C. chopped onion

Place the Lentil Soup Mix in a large soup pot. Add 9 cups water and bring to a boil. Add the vegetables and simmer the soup partially covered for 2 hours or until the lentils are soft.

Lentil Soup

1 jar Lentil Soup Mix
4 carrots, diced

4 stalks celery, diced
1 C. chopped onion

Place the Lentil Soup Mix in a large soup pot. Add 9 cups water and bring to a boil. Add the vegetables and simmer the soup partially covered for 2 hours or until the lentils are soft.

Lentil Soup

1 jar Lentil Soup Mix
4 carrots, diced

4 stalks celery, diced
1 C. chopped onion

Place the Lentil Soup Mix in a large soup pot. Add 9 cups water and bring to a boil. Add the vegetables and simmer the soup partially covered for 2 hours or until the lentils are soft.

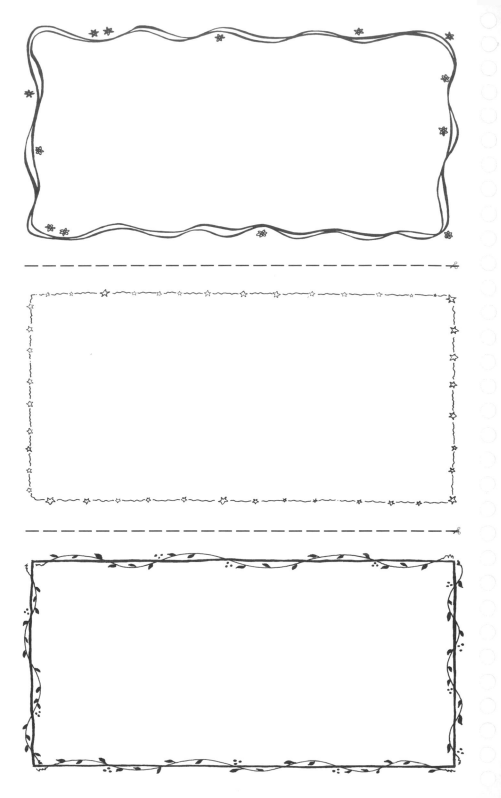

Lentil Soup

1 jar Lentil Soup Mix
4 carrots, diced

4 stalks celery, diced
1 C. chopped onion

Place the Lentil Soup Mix in a large soup pot. Add 9 cups water and bring to a boil. Add the vegetables and simmer the soup partially covered for 2 hours or until the lentils are soft.

Lentil Soup

1 jar Lentil Soup Mix
4 carrots, diced

4 stalks celery, diced
1 C. chopped onion

Place the Lentil Soup Mix in a large soup pot. Add 9 cups water and bring to a boil. Add the vegetables and simmer the soup partially covered for 2 hours or until the lentils are soft.

Lentil Soup

1 jar Lentil Soup Mix
4 carrots, diced

4 stalks celery, diced
1 C. chopped onion

Place the Lentil Soup Mix in a large soup pot. Add 9 cups water and bring to a boil. Add the vegetables and simmer the soup partially covered for 2 hours or until the lentils are soft.

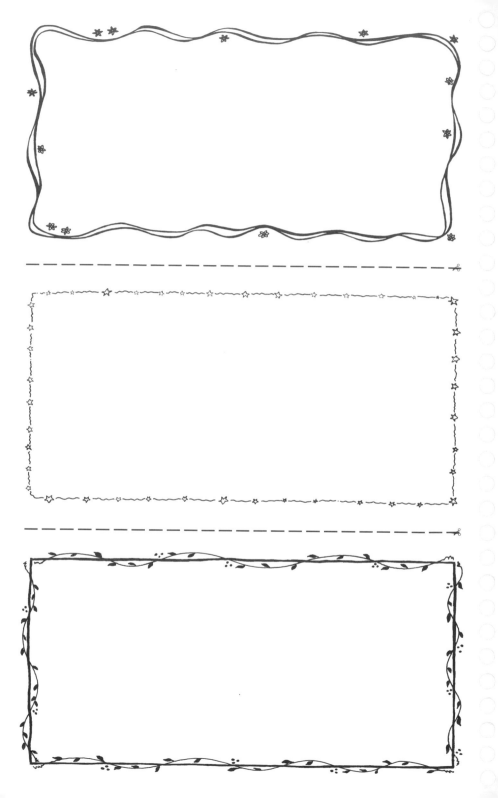

Curly Soup Mix

2 T. dried parsley flakes
1 tsp. pepper
2 T. beef bouillon granules
1/3 C. dried minced onion
1 tsp. sugar
3 to 3 1/2 C. tri-colored curly
    rotini pasta spirals, optional
    to divide by color

Layer the ingredients in the order given into a wide-mouth 1-quart canning jar. Pack each layer in place before adding the next ingredient.

Attach a gift tag with the cooking directions.

❀ *For a different look, place a small amount of stuffing under a fabric cover before attaching to "puff" the top.* ❀

Curly Soup

1 jar Curly Soup Mix
1 (14 ounce) can crushed or
   diced tomatoes

Bring 8 cups of water to a boil in a large soup pot. Add the Curly Soup Mix and tomatoes. Bring back to a boil. Lower heat and simmer uncovered for 12 to 15 minutes until pasta is tender.

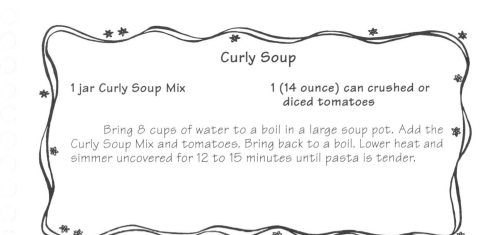

Curly Soup

1 jar Curly Soup Mix

1 (14 ounce) can crushed or
diced tomatoes

Bring 8 cups of water to a boil in a large soup pot. Add the
Curly Soup Mix and tomatoes. Bring back to a boil. Lower heat and
simmer uncovered for 12 to 15 minutes until pasta is tender.

Curly Soup

1 jar Curly Soup Mix

1 (14 ounce) can crushed or
diced tomatoes

Bring 8 cups of water to a boil in a large soup pot. Add the
Curly Soup Mix and tomatoes. Bring back to a boil. Lower heat and
simmer uncovered for 12 to 15 minutes until pasta is tender.

Curly Soup

1 jar Curly Soup Mix

1 (14 ounce) can crushed or
diced tomatoes

Bring 8 cups of water to a boil in a large soup pot. Add the
Curly Soup Mix and tomatoes. Bring back to a boil. Lower heat and
simmer uncovered for 12 to 15 minutes until pasta is tender.

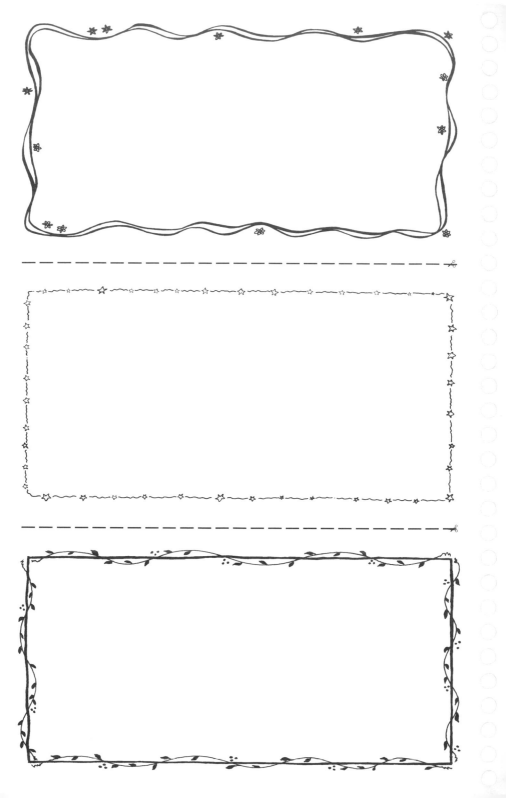

Curly Soup

1 jar Curly Soup Mix

1 (14 ounce) can crushed or
diced tomatoes

Bring 8 cups of water to a boil in a large soup pot. Add the Curly Soup Mix and tomatoes. Bring back to a boil. Lower heat and simmer uncovered for 12 to 15 minutes until pasta is tender.

Curly Soup

1 jar Curly Soup Mix

1 (14 ounce) can crushed or
diced tomatoes

Bring 8 cups of water to a boil in a large soup pot. Add the Curly Soup Mix and tomatoes. Bring back to a boil. Lower heat and simmer uncovered for 12 to 15 minutes until pasta is tender.

Curly Soup

1 jar Curly Soup Mix

1 (14 ounce) can crushed or
diced tomatoes

Bring 8 cups of water to a boil in a large soup pot. Add the Curly Soup Mix and tomatoes. Bring back to a boil. Lower heat and simmer uncovered for 12 to 15 minutes until pasta is tender.

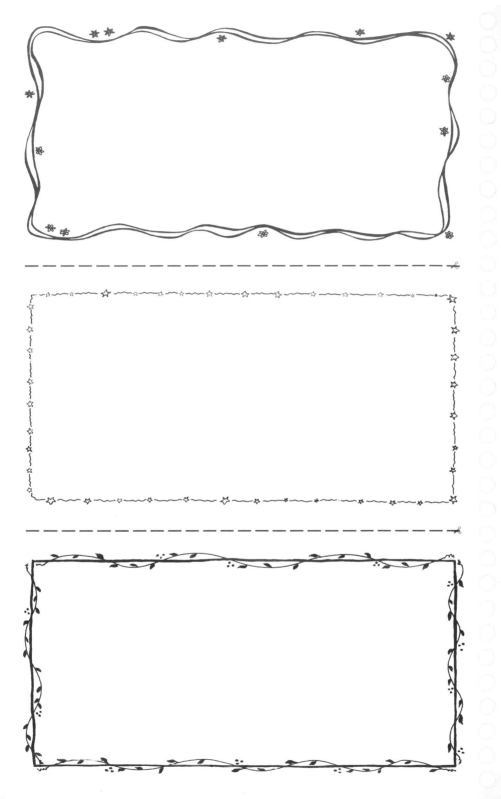

Minestrone Soup Mix

1/2 C. dried split peas
1 C. dried kidney beans
8 crumbled beef bouillon
   cubes
2 tsp. dried basil
2 tsp. dried oregano
2 tsp. dried parsley
1 T. salt
1 tsp. pepper
2 C. elbow macaroni, wrapped
   in plastic wrap

Layer the ingredients in the order given into a wide-mouth 1-quart canning jar. Pack each layer in place before adding the next ingredient.

Attach a gift tag with the cooking directions.

Fill a soup gift basket with a soup jar mixes, crackers, a big soup mug, and a journal.

Minestrone Soup

1 jar Minestrone Soup Mix
2 pounds sweet Italian
   sausage
4 carrots, diced
4 stalks celery, diced
1 C. chopped onion
2 (28 ounce) cans diced
tomatoes

Remove the elbow macaroni from the Minestrone Soup Mix and set aside. Place the balance of the mix in a large soup pot. Add 16 cups of water and simmer for 1 1/2 hours. Remove the skin from the sausage. In a skillet, brown the sausage, breaking it into small pieces. Add the vegetables to the skillet and sauté for 3 to 5 minutes. Add the sausage, vegetables and tomatoes to the soup. Bring the soup to a boil, and add the elbow macaroni. Simmer for 30 minutes.

Minestrone Soup

1 jar Minestrone Soup Mix
2 pounds sweet Italian sausage
4 carrots, diced

4 stalks celery, diced
1 C. chopped onion
2 (28 ounce) cans diced
tomatoes

Remove the elbow macaroni from the Minestrone Soup Mix and set aside. Place the balance of the mix in a large soup pot. Add 16 cups of water and simmer for 1 1/2 hours. Remove the skin from the sausage. In a skillet, brown the sausage, breaking it into small pieces. Add the vegetables to the skillet and sauté for 3 to 5 minutes. Add the sausage, vegetables and tomatoes to the soup. Bring the soup to a boil, and add the elbow macaroni. Simmer for 30 minutes.

Minestrone Soup

1 jar Minestrone Soup Mix
2 pounds sweet Italian sausage
4 carrots, diced

4 stalks celery, diced
1 C. chopped onion
2 (28 ounce) cans diced
tomatoes

Remove the elbow macaroni from the Minestrone Soup Mix and set aside. Place the balance of the mix in a large soup pot. Add 16 cups of water and simmer for 1 1/2 hours. Remove the skin from the sausage. In a skillet, brown the sausage, breaking it into small pieces. Add the vegetables to the skillet and sauté for 3 to 5 minutes. Add the sausage, vegetables and tomatoes to the soup. Bring the soup to a boil, and add the elbow macaroni. Simmer for 30 minutes.

Minestrone Soup

1 jar Minestrone Soup Mix
2 pounds sweet Italian sausage
4 carrots, diced

4 stalks celery, diced
1 C. chopped onion
2 (28 ounce) cans diced
tomatoes

Remove the elbow macaroni from the Minestrone Soup Mix and set aside. Place the balance of the mix in a large soup pot. Add 16 cups of water and simmer for 1 1/2 hours. Remove the skin from the sausage. In a skillet, brown the sausage, breaking it into small pieces. Add the vegetables to the skillet and sauté for 3 to 5 minutes. Add the sausage, vegetables and tomatoes to the soup. Bring the soup to a boil, and add the elbow macaroni. Simmer for 30 minutes.

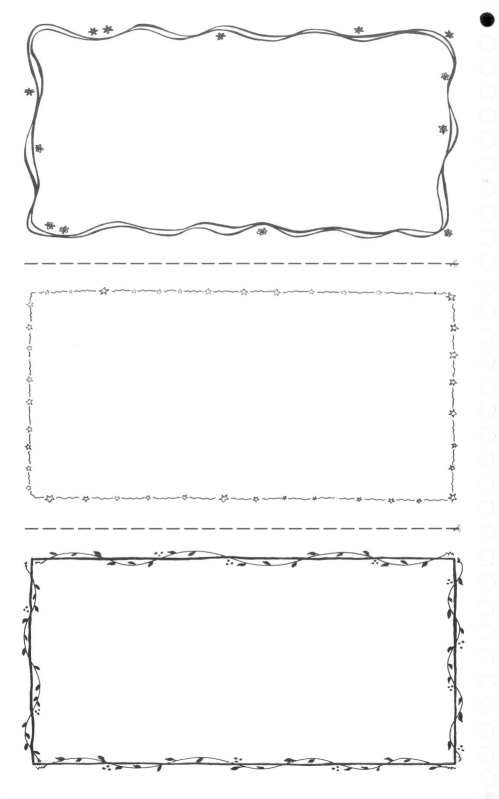

Minestrone Soup

1 jar Minestrone Soup Mix
2 pounds sweet Italian sausage
4 carrots, diced

4 stalks celery, diced
1 C. chopped onion
2 (28 ounce) cans diced tomatoes

Remove the elbow macaroni from the Minestrone Soup Mix and set aside. Place the balance of the mix in a large soup pot. Add 16 cups of water and simmer for 1 1/2 hours. Remove the skin from the sausage. In a skillet, brown the sausage, breaking it into small pieces. Add the vegetables to the skillet and sauté for 3 to 5 minutes. Add the sausage, vegetables and tomatoes to the soup. Bring the soup to a boil, and add the elbow macaroni. Simmer for 30 minutes.

Minestrone Soup

1 jar Minestrone Soup Mix
2 pounds sweet Italian sausage
4 carrots, diced

4 stalks celery, diced
1 C. chopped onion
2 (28 ounce) cans diced tomatoes

Remove the elbow macaroni from the Minestrone Soup Mix and set aside. Place the balance of the mix in a large soup pot. Add 16 cups of water and simmer for 1 1/2 hours. Remove the skin from the sausage. In a skillet, brown the sausage, breaking it into small pieces. Add the vegetables to the skillet and sauté for 3 to 5 minutes. Add the sausage, vegetables and tomatoes to the soup. Bring the soup to a boil, and add the elbow macaroni. Simmer for 30 minutes.

Minestrone Soup

1 jar Minestrone Soup Mix
2 pounds sweet Italian sausage
4 carrots, diced

4 stalks celery, diced
1 C. chopped onion
2 (28 ounce) cans diced tomatoes

Remove the elbow macaroni from the Minestrone Soup Mix and set aside. Place the balance of the mix in a large soup pot. Add 16 cups of water and simmer for 1 1/2 hours. Remove the skin from the sausage. In a skillet, brown the sausage, breaking it into small pieces. Add the vegetables to the skillet and sauté for 3 to 5 minutes. Add the sausage, vegetables and tomatoes to the soup. Bring the soup to a boil, and add the elbow macaroni. Simmer for 30 minutes.

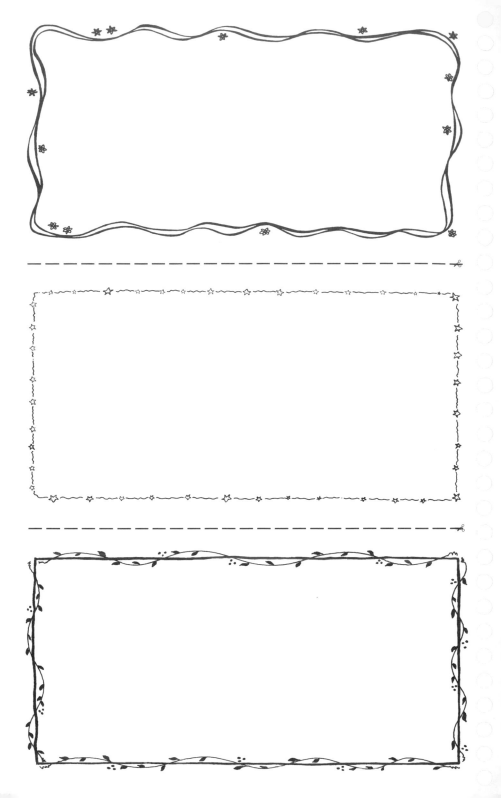

Peas and Barley Soup Mix

1 C. green split peas
1 C. lentils
1 T. salt
1 T. garlic powder
1 C. pearl barley
3/4 C. macaroni or brown rice
1/4 C. celery flakes
1/4 C. parsley flakes
1/2 tsp. thyme
1/2 tsp. pepper

Layer the ingredients in the order given into a wide-mouth 1-quart canning jar. Pack each layer in place before adding the next ingredient.

Attach a gift tag with the cooking directions.

❀ To make a gift in a jar fancier, decorate it with a doily and ribbon. ❀

Peas and Barley Soup

1 jar Peas and Barley Soup Mix
4 C. chopped, cooked meat, as
    desired

    Place Peas and Barley Soup Mix in a large soup pot. Add 16 cups of water and meat, as desired. Bring to a boil. Reduce heat to low and cover pan. Simmer for 45 to 50 minutes, or until peas are tender.

Peas and Barley Soup

1 jar Peas and Barley Soup Mix 4 C. chopped, cooked meat, as desired

Place Peas and Barley Soup Mix in a large soup pot. Add 16 cups of water and meat, as desired. Bring to a boil. Reduce heat to low and cover pan. Simmer for 45 to 50 minutes, or until peas are tender.

Peas and Barley Soup

1 jar Peas and Barley Soup Mix 4 C. chopped, cooked meat, as desired

Place Peas and Barley Soup Mix in a large soup pot. Add 16 cups of water and meat, as desired. Bring to a boil. Reduce heat to low and cover pan. Simmer for 45 to 50 minutes, or until peas are tender.

Peas and Barley Soup

1 jar Peas and Barley Soup Mix 4 C. chopped, cooked meat, as desired

Place Peas and Barley Soup Mix in a large soup pot. Add 16 cups of water and meat, as desired. Bring to a boil. Reduce heat to low and cover pan. Simmer for 45 to 50 minutes, or until peas are tender.

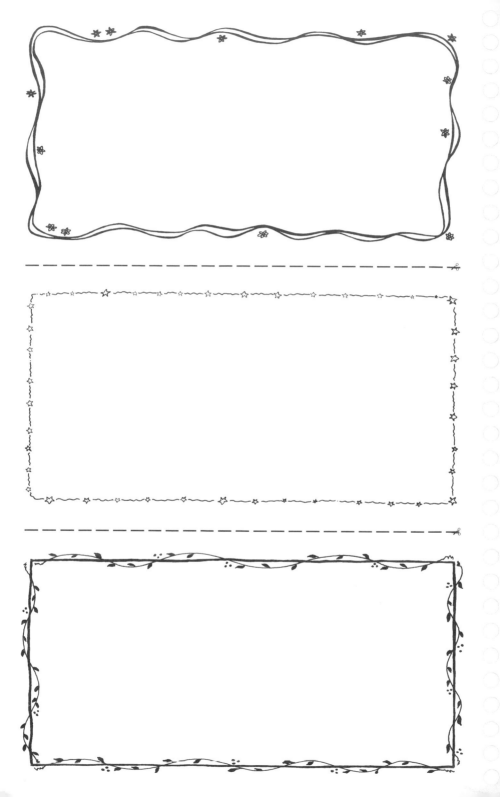

Peas and Barley Soup

1 jar Peas and Barley Soup Mix

4 C. chopped, cooked meat, as desired

Place Peas and Barley Soup Mix in a large soup pot. Add 16 cups of water and meat, as desired. Bring to a boil. Reduce heat to low and cover pan. Simmer for 45 to 50 minutes, or until peas are tender.

Peas and Barley Soup

1 jar Peas and Barley Soup Mix

4 C. chopped, cooked meat, as desired

Place Peas and Barley Soup Mix in a large soup pot. Add 16 cups of water and meat, as desired. Bring to a boil. Reduce heat to low and cover pan. Simmer for 45 to 50 minutes, or until peas are tender.

Peas and Barley Soup

1 jar Peas and Barley Soup Mix

4 C. chopped, cooked meat, as desired

Place Peas and Barley Soup Mix in a large soup pot. Add 16 cups of water and meat, as desired. Bring to a boil. Reduce heat to low and cover pan. Simmer for 45 to 50 minutes, or until peas are tender.

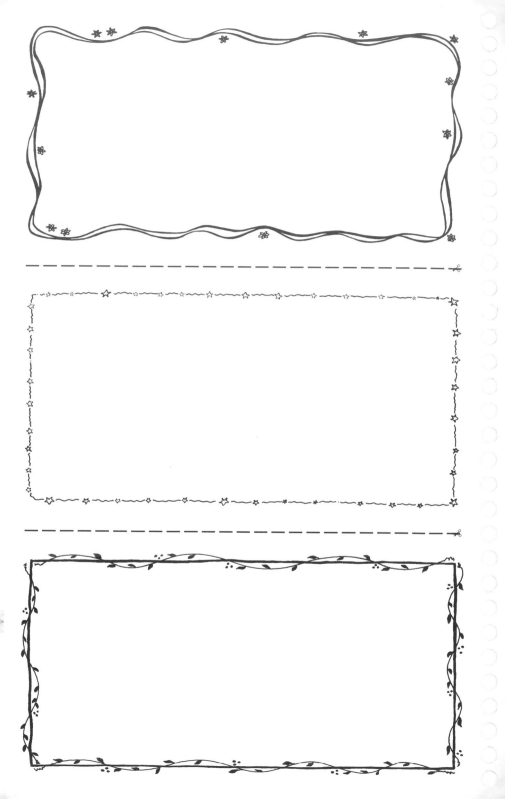